# HISTORIC INDIANAPOLIS CRIMES

FRED D. CAVINDER

# HISTORIC INDIANAPOLIS CRIMES

MURDER
+ MYSTERY
IN THE
CIRCLE CITY

THE
History
PRESS

Published by The History Press
Charleston, SC 29403
www.historypress.net

Copyright © 2010 by Fred D. Cavinder
All rights reserved

First published 2010
Second printing 2012

Manufactured in the United States

ISBN 978.1.59629.989.4

Cavinder, Fred D., 1931-
Historic Indianapolis crimes : murder and mystery in the Circle City / Fred D. Cavinder.
p. cm.
ISBN 978-1-59629-989-4
1. Murder--Indiana--Indianapolis--History. 2. Murderers--Indiana--Indianapolis--History.
3. Murder victims--Indiana--History. I. Title.
HV6534.I6C38 2010
364.152'30977252--dc22
2010020426

# CONTENTS

# CONTENTS

# INTRODUCTION

Indianapolis patrolman Hugh Burns was off duty one evening in the summer of 1883 when a citizen approached him about an argument underway in a nearby boardinghouse. The supplicant knew that Burns was a cop. As Burns entered, the argument became physical, and one of the participants, John Jeter of Kentucky, pulled a weapon and shot Burns to death. Jeter escaped punishment, contending that he didn't know Burns was a policeman. Burns was the first Indianapolis policeman murdered in the line of duty, but he was not the last, and civilians in the capital had been homicide victims for years before Burns died.

The first murder in the city, then a mere fraction of its later size, occurred in the 1830s, and slayings never have stopped. Because of its size, the city is destined to be the capital of Hoosier homicides—growing population does that. Yet, with one possible exception, the Indiana capital has never experienced serial killers or endured the drama and fear of, say, Son of Sam.

Some homicides stir the public. Cases in point are the heartless torture and slaying of Sylvia Likens and the Indianapolis massacre of seven, including children. The public seems to register limited concern about many killings; television dulls murders as they come into your living room nightly on both the news and crime dramas. On TV programs, the killer is caught within an hour via state-of-the-art tools used almost instantaneously by actor-investigators; sometimes they employ computer magic that exists only in the minds of writers.

In real life, some killers are the stuff of legend—Jack the Ripper comes to mind—and some so-called killers are legendary in Indiana criminal annals. Luminary bandit John H. Dillinger was born in Indianapolis. Despite his shoot-it-out image, he was accused of only one slaying—the death of East Chicago policeman William P. O'Malley. Some think it perhaps wasn't Dillinger's shot at all.

In Dillinger's day and before, slayings were simpler; in a sense, they were old-fashioned murders: for hire, slayings of passion, homicides for retribution, killings to eliminate witnesses and collateral damage. Today, these motives are often eclipsed by the slayings in drug deals gone bad, drug-high homicides and drive-by shootings. Not only are the gunmen often unknown, but sometimes the identity of the real intended victim also remains uncertain.

Homicides gain added sensation when the killer escapes justice. Murder does not always out, despite what the novelists and forensic scientists tell you. The era has a lot to do with it; years ago, DNA evidence and other investigative techniques and technologies didn't exist. The most notorious unsolved crimes of old created a cult of curiosity; newspapers and magazines routinely dig up anniversary angles to rehash the still mysterious homicides.

Deciding on intriguing homicides obviously involves extensive selectivity. Should the followers of Hoosier Jim Jones in Guyana be included? Hoosier Jones began his tragic course after founding the People's Temple in Indianapolis. Certainly the deaths of nine hundred of his followers in Guyana were homicides. Obviously, the gunmen who shot some of the victims were killers. Jones's participation presents a fine point; convincing others to kill themselves differs marginally from applying the poison yourself. Jones was cruel, controlling and probably delusional. But his role as a murderer is best left to philosophers and, possibly, theologians.

Obviously, parameters must be narrower than that.

Murdered policemen are a special category; the job puts them in harm's way. One might typify Indianapolis police killings with three cases—one shockingly brutal, from the 1930s era of bandits; another a landmark in murder punishments; and a third that launched one of the biggest manhunts in Indianapolis history. Let these police murders, then, serve as templates for Indianapolis police slayings.

Material for this book has been collected from files of the *Indianapolis Star* and the now-defunct *Indianapolis News* and *Indianapolis Times*, from some now-defunct weekly Indianapolis newspapers, from historical documents such as the Oberholtzer confession and, in a few cases, from books about individual murders: *The Indiana Torture Slaying* by John Dean (1966), *My Indiana* by Irving Liebowitz and *In the Eyes of the Law* by Tom Faulconer.

# Part I

# Lethal for the Law

## Making Dillinger Look Like a Piker

Dr. Emmett Rose was out on a call the afternoon of April 27, 1936, when a man approached his wife in their Indianapolis home-office near Garfield Park.

Mrs. Rose was suspicious. The caller said that a friend had been shot because he had been running around with another man's wife. Not so unusual in itself. But the wounded man was being helped by his three companions from a car with Illinois license plates. "I thought it strange someone should bring a wounded man all the way from Illinois for my husband to treat," she said later. When assured that the doctor would not return for some time, the men drove away.

When he returned and heard what had happened, the doctor told his wife to call the police. The police told her that if the men returned she should call again.

Later that day, Mrs. Rose peeked into her husband's office and saw him talking to the man who had been there earlier. The expression on Dr. Rose's face served as a warning to her, and she retreated out the back door of the house at 2153 Barth Avenue. Although the men in the parked car saw her speed to a nearby drugstore, they took no action. "I don't know why they didn't shoot me, but they didn't," she said. At the drugstore, she asked the clerk to call police.

The men Mrs. Rose was dealing with, although she didn't know it, were the Brady gang, which had been formulated the year before in an Indianapolis

*Above*: Al Brady's police mug shot was taken during the days his gang terrorized Indiana and elsewhere. *Indianapolis Police Department files.*

*Left*: Indianapolis sergeant Richard Rivers was gunned down near Garfield Park. *Indianapolis Police Department files.*

garage. Al Brady, born in Goodland, Indiana, was neglected, orphaned at sixteen and imprisoned for burglary. In prison, he determined to become a better criminal. He hooked up with James Dalhover, a fellow inmate from Cincinnati, who had a record for making illegal liquor, stealing cars and committing assaults. In October 1935, they were joined by Clarence Lee Shaffer Jr. of Indianapolis, who by age twelve had been arrested for stealing cars and stripping them. Shaffer induced Rhuel Charles Giesking, also of Indianapolis, to later join the gang.

In January, the initial trio met in a garage on Park Avenue in Indianapolis, where they mounted a machine gun on a steel tripod. "Dillinger never had anything like this," Brady is believed to have said. They set out on their crime spree, holding up jewelry stores and big food markets on Saturday nights.

At a jewelry store in Lima, Ohio, three went inside and left Dalhover on alert in the car. When he saw policeman Jess Ford park a patrol car nearby and climb out of it, Dalhover jumped out, gun in hand, and confronted Ford. But Ford's partner saw the confrontation from a restaurant window while he was dining. This policeman, E.O. Swaney, ran out shooting. In the ensuing battle, both policemen were wounded by machine gun fire, and

Brady gangster James Dalhover (left) was executed; Clarence Shaffer was killed by the FBI. *Indianapolis Police Department files.*

This is the house where Brady gang member Rhuel Giesking was taken for treatment. *Photo by author.*

Giesking was winged by a bullet that passed through one leg and lodged in the other. The gang escaped.

Giesking was the wounded man Dr. Rose was being asked to treat. By that time, the slug had been in Giesking's leg for a month.

When the drugstore clerk alerted by Mrs. Rose called police, Sergeant Richard Rivers, patrolling near the Barth Avenue address, got the run. He parked in the alley behind Dr. Rose's house. When he reached the front porch and started to enter, he was cut down by a blaze of machine gun bullets from the car. Sergeant Rivers died almost instantly. Al Brady, the man who had been talking to Dr. Rose, fled the house, revolver in hand, and jumped in the car, which sped away. Police agencies all over the Midwest were alerted. The gang headed for Chicago.

In the Lima shootout, Brady had dropped the card of a fence they used in Chicago, and that gave away the gang. When cornered in Chicago, Brady

Patrolman Rivers had this view from the alley where he parked; he was slain at the entrance to the house. *Photo by author.*

withheld gunfire, possibly because of a blonde who was with him. Captured, he was returned to Indianapolis. The fence also helped to identify Dalhover's girlfriend. Police seized him. A tipster led police to Shaffer, found reading a magazine in his Indianapolis home.

When Brad, Dalhover and Shaffer were indicted, their attorney obtained a change of venue to Hancock County, and the three were transferred to the Greenfield jail. The trio loosened rivets in a yard-long steel bar in their cell, and when Hancock County sheriff Clarence Watson came in with their meal on October 11, they clubbed him and escaped in a commandeered Chevy. They began a series of bank robberies in four midwestern states, killing at least three citizens.

On May 27, 1937, the gangsters hit the bank in Goodland, Brady's hometown, for $4,000 and fled in a maroon sedan. With main roads blocked, Indiana state trooper Paul Minneman and Deputy Sheriff Elmer Craig began searching. They spotted the maroon sedan parked behind a church in northeast White County.

When Minneman stepped from the car, he was mowed down as part of gunfire and died sixty-four hours later. The deputy sheriff was wounded but survived. The Federal Bureau of Investigation (FBI) joined in searching for the gang; they were on the Ten Most Wanted list.

On October 12, 1937, a year and a day after the three gangsters had escaped jail in Greenfield, FBI agents cornered them in Bangor, Maine. They were traced there through an order for a gun they had placed with a sports store. But when the gangsters arrived at the store, an FBI agent was posing as a clerk. He crushed Dalhover's skull with a gun butt. Shaffer and Brady, outside in the car, started blazing with guns.

Brady fired four times with Minneman's revolver before being fatally wounded. Shaffer was killed while trying to escape. Dalhover surrendered. He was returned to Indianapolis, tried for the murder of Sergeant Rivers and executed under a federal warrant on December 13, 1938. Giesking, who eventually had to go to a hospital, was also captured. The disposition of his case seems to be unknown.

Some in Indiana were disturbed that Brady was buried in a pauper's grave in Maine. Most of the gang's robberies had been in Indiana, and Hoosier lawmen felt cheated that the gang had been brought to justice in New England.

# The "Madman" Murderer

It was a savage slaying by any measure. Seven slugs from a .45-caliber army automatic penetrated the victim's heart, spleen, liver, right lung, left wrist, waist and chest. When the dead man turned out to be a Marion County deputy sheriff, the city of Indianapolis was galvanized and one thousand lawmen hunted the killer.

On that April 16, 1961 morning, Indianapolis did not yet encompass all of Marion County, and city police and sheriff's deputies had not merged. So twenty-three-year-old Deputy Edward G. Byrne was on duty on the far east side of the county when he was shot down.

Not long after his body was found, police knew who they sought—two partners of the murderer had given him up, admitting only to burglary. "He's a madman," one of them said of the shooter. "I'm a burglar. I don't go for that gun junk."

The "madman" was Michael Thomas Callahan, and the manhunt was on. Callahan had told associates that he would "go south" if he ever got hot. Soon, tips to police put him about thirty miles south of Indianapolis. There, despite some concerns that he would kill himself to avoid capture, he was seized two and a half days later without incident, lowered head-first through an attic hole.

It took four later trials to finally convict the thirty-six-year-old Callahan, already a veteran of years behind bars. Then the death sentence was changed to life in prison. Because of quirks in the law at that time, Callahan was almost eligible for parole by the time the life sentence was imposed.

Byrne, a member of the force less than a year and only fifteen days into patrol duty, was two hours into his Sunday morning shift. A call to the sheriff's office reported the burglar alarm going off at the Hilltop Tavern in far east Marion County. The owner of a nearby hardware store said that he had heard the alarm and saw men coming out of the tavern. Byrne talked to the hardware owner Raymond Grimes and then headed toward the tavern on Tenth Street.

He spotted a 1958 Oldsmobile pulling away from the tavern and pulled it over. Three men got out of the car. One of them seemed to try to obscure the Oldsmobile's license plate, while the other two stood beside the patrol car. When Byrne asked the man to move away from the plate, he instead walked to the window of the patrol car and, as Byrne picked up his radio mike, said, "Forget it. You're dead."

Ironically, Indianapolis city patrolman John R. Kennedy heard the fatal shots from the driveway of his house about two hundred yards from the altercation.

Deputy Ed Byrne met death during a traffic stop. *Marion County Sheriff's Department files.*

When he saw the men trying to move their car, he thought the deputy was helping them and dismissed the sounds as car backfires. When he checked a few minutes later, the Oldsmobile was gone and Byrne was dead. Other arriving police officers found the murder weapon in the mud at the scene.

Sergeant Thomas Klein, one of many lawmen combing the city, saw a man known to be a burglar parked outside an Indianapolis apartment near downtown; a companion ran into the apartments. Klein picked up James William Walker Jr., and he soon implicated Ralph Eugene DuBois; they told how Callahan had shot down Byrne like a dog. DuBois termed Callahan "a madman."

Investigation revealed that Callahan had a prison record, arrests on other charges for which he was out on bond, was probably armed with a sawed-off shotgun and a revolver and, despite being considered somewhat mild mannered, was capable of anything. He was five feet, ten and a half inches tall, 220 pounds, wearing a crew cut and had a fat face that had earned him the nickname "Hoghead"; he also used barbiturates. His forty-year-old wife Dorothy said that she feared he might kill himself to avoid having to return to prison. Callahan had a dry cleaning business in Indianapolis and was a

The *Indianapolis News* detailed the capture of Michael Callahan (center) with a series of photos.

talented tailor, an outgrowth of working in the tailor shop at the Indiana Reformatory at Pendleton. He had spent two sentences at the reformatory, one stemming from a 1948 arrest for service station burglaries.

City police and deputies combed Marion County, three to a patrol car. Callahan was considered too dangerous to be approached by only two. As Deputy Byrne was being laid to rest at an east-side cemetery about 3:00 p.m. on April 18, tips placed Callahan in a house near the town of Bargersville. He reportedly had been seen being driven in that direction by a friend. A posse—some lawmen left the Byrne services to take part—assembled and began a military-like operation, starting with an encompassing circle of more than twenty lawmen nearly one mile wide. A helicopter hovered. Converging on the one-story house, lawmen found it seemingly empty, but one—State Police sergeant Jay H. Romack—saw a scratch on a heater under a sixteen-inch hole leading into the attic. In the attic, he encountered Callahan. With the warning "I'll blow your head off," Romack seized Callahan, handcuffed him and dropped him head-first down to other waiting police.

When Callahan was returned to Indianapolis and confronted with Walker and DuBois, he denied knowing anything about the killing, saying that he wasn't even there and claiming that his accusers were high on drugs. But the continual insistence of his partners in crime led to indictments on all three, as well as other fallout.

For one thing, DuBois said that he had witnessed Callahan shoot two other men in the commission of robberies; one had been shot with the same .45 that killed Byrne, DuBois said. He and his wife, Jean, had worked at Callahan's dry cleaning shop, which was believed to have been a front for the burglary operation in which Callahan was involved. DuBois also said that he had been involved in the burglary of four hundred houses and two hundred stores, most of them with Callahan. The duo had been seized in one tavern robbery, but the case had not yet been adjudicated. Callahan also had been under three charges, but his bond had been reduced for some unknown reason. A retainer that would have moved him to federal

Ed Byrne's murder followed a burglary at this tavern, which still stands only blocks from the slaying site. *Photo by author.*

jurisdiction on charges of robbery and auto banditry seemingly had not reached local authorities, so Callahan was released from jail the day before Byrne lost his life.

Police had also seized Arthur E. Ingram. He was the owner of the house in which Callahan had holed up. Ingram was later released because police said that they had insufficient evidence to prosecute him for aiding a criminal.

Callahan, through various appeals, had three trials before the death penalty option was taken off the table. He was held in the Indiana Reformatory at Pendleton until 1976. He had been taken there for safekeeping, lest he and Walker and DuBois stir too much unrest if all were in the Marion County Jail.

Callahan's life sentence was imposed on January 6, 1976, by Judge David T. Woods after conviction in Brown Circuit Court, where the case had been taken upon a change of venue. Callahan's case had been overturned by a federal court in 1962, and two subsequent trials had resulted in a hung jury and a mistrial.

By the time Callahan was given life, DuBois had served thirteen years for his role in the Byrnes case and Walker had died in prison. So the murder of Ed Byrnes had taken almost fifteen years to be resolved.

# Murder Aftermaths

The slaying of Indianapolis detective Jack R. Ohrberg in an early morning confrontation while he was trying to serve a warrant resulted in two historical events. One of the men convicted in Ohrberg's killing would become the last put to death in the electric chair in Indiana. The second man convicted in the murder would become the first executed by lethal injection in the state. Both defendants would be part of a firestorm of criticism involving the facts of the case and the death penalty in Indiana.

The scenario began about 5:30 a.m. on December 11, 1980, on the northeast side of Indianapolis. Detectives, led by Ohrberg, had been investigating a cold case, the August 4 slaying of Brink's guard William E. Sieg Jr. at a department store.

Some $50,000 had been taken in the Brink's robbery, and for a time leads had dried up, despite a reward of $100,000. But during lulls in the Indianapolis crime scene, Ohrberg and other homicide detectives had renewed the investigation, and "they received phone calls and people began to talk," Ohrberg's commander said. Suspected were Earl Resnover, twenty-eight; his brother Gregory D. Resnover, twenty-nine; and an associate named Tommie J. Smith, twenty-six, sometimes called Mr. P. or "the Priest." They also were suspects in the February 6 armed robbery of an Indianapolis bank across town.

Ohrberg, who was not wearing a bulletproof vest, approached an Oxford Street address with two other detectives; they had arrest warrants. He knocked on the door and identified the trio as policemen. Getting no response, they asked a neighbor if anyone was at home. The neighbor said that there had been noise in the house.

Ohrberg returned to the porch and banged on the door with his shoulder; it yielded slightly. There was furniture blocking the door. Two or three muzzle flashes occurred inside the house. "I've been hit," Ohrberg called out. "Get help." Then, according to testimony, someone leaned out of the partly opened door and fired several times. Ohrberg was hit again. The five remaining police scattered; an ambulance and backup were summoned.

There were numerous shots fired. At last, Gregory Resnover came out, threw down an AR-15 rifle, an automatic military weapon, and surrendered. Earl Resnover did the same, surrendering another AR-15 rifle and a pistol. Two women also gave up. They were identified as Teresa L. Nance and Samara Y. Palmer. Inside, police found Tommie Smith wounded and bleeding. Beside him was a third AR-15, later determined to be the weapon with which Ohrberg was shot. Smith was transported to the hospital, where he eventually recovered.

Several weapons were seized, including handguns, an M-1 rifle that was tossed onto the lawn and a fourth AR-15. Clips for the weapons contained as many as forty rounds of ammunition. A total of two hundred rounds of ammo was found in the house, along with bulletproof vests.

Ohrberg, forty-four and a lanky nineteen-year veteran, was the forty-sixth Indianapolis policeman slain in the line of duty. The circumstances of his slaying required little investigation. The five persons in the house were all charged with murder or being accessories. A third woman, Linda E. Jones, was charged with assisting a criminal, accused of helping Earl Resnover when he was wounded during the Brinks job.

Soon, rumors circulated that Ohrberg had been targeted for killing and that then Indianapolis prosecutor Stephen Goldsmith was on an assassination list. Ohrberg's business card was found on Earl Resnover. It turned out that Ohrberg had given the card to Resnover's mother during the investigation.

It was learned that Tommie Smith was wanted in Grant County on several charges from 1979. In a startling development, Princess A. Dale, twenty-one, was arrested at her desk in police headquarters, charged with assisting a criminal. Dale was a cousin of the Resnovers and worked as a statistician and clerk in the team policing division. She was accused of giving her cousins copies of police reports concerning the bank robbery investigation.

The trial of Smith and Gregory Resnover drew to a conclusion after seven days of testimony at the end of June 1981, including a rare Sunday session. About 5:30 p.m. on Monday, June 29, verdicts of guilty were handed down by the jury of eight men and four women after five and a half hours of deliberation. The pair was also charged with conspiracy. Those two, plus Earl Resnover, still faced charges of murder in the slaying of the Brink's guard.

The contention of the defense during the trial was that the occupants of the house on Oxford Street were sleeping when the detectives arrived and did not know that it was the police pounding on their door; they fired "at an intruder."

On Tuesday, Smith and Gregory Resnover boycotted a sentencing hearing. On July 23, each was sentenced to die by Judge Jeffrey V. Boles of Hendricks Circuit Court. The case was first moved to Hendricks County and, by agreement, was returned to Marion County, with Boles presiding. The sentence was in keeping with the Indiana law concerning a policeman slain in the line of duty.

On September 29, 1981, Smith, Gregory Resnover and Earl Resnover were found guilty of the killing of Brink's guard Sieg, who had been shot twice while carrying cash in a Kmart store in Indianapolis. Several witnesses identified the trio. An accomplice testified that the robbery plan included the premise that it would not succeed unless the guard was slain. Each defendant was sentenced to eighty years in prison in that case.

Gregory Resnover had changed his name to Ajamu Nassor, and Tommie Smith had changed his name to Ziyon Yisrayah; efforts were launched to save them from execution. An estimated forty thousand people wrote then governor Evan Bayh. Appeals through the courts failed, as did campaigns by death penalty foes, including the Human Rights Coalition of Indiana. On Wednesday, December 7, 1994, TV trucks from all over the Midwest and numerous newspaper reporters descended on Indiana State Prison at Michigan City. Thirteen minutes after midnight the next day, Resnover was executed in the electric chair, the third since the death penalty had been reinstated in 1977 and the last to die by that means.

Smith, too, instituted numerous appeals, had several stays and was denied clemency by Governor Bayh. He was executed by lethal injection, pronounced dead at 1:23 a.m. on July 19, 1996, the seventy-fourth convicted murderer executed in Indiana since 1900.

# Part II

# Vintage Violence

## Was It or Wasn't It?

The first murder in Indianapolis may have been an accident, although a murder charge was filed. The auxiliary to the case was an unfulfilled love affair.

William McPherson was a suitor of Mary Barbee's, a much-sought-after, black-haired, pink-cheeked beauty who lived with her aunt in a large house facing Meridian Street in the area where the Federal Building stands today. The property of the aunt, Mrs. John G. Brown, included an arbor, which was the scene of romantic rendezvous.

McPherson was a timekeeper and clerk for William H. Wernwag, a contractor who was building the Washington Street bridge across the White River in the early 1830s. McPherson was well dressed and debonair, widely acquainted and well liked, but he was somehow the subject of scandalous rumors. Early Indianapolis histories noted that he had been accused of "licentious habits and intrigues."

Despite that, Mary Barbee accepted a ring of rubies and pearls from him. But her family, perhaps because of the rumors, did not look favorably on McPherson, and he and Mary drifted apart. In a letter, McPherson said that he realized he lacked the approval of Mary's family and feared that his continued attention might embarrass her. But, the note said, if she really loved him, nothing else would have mattered.

Mary Barbee sent a reply, and the day after McPherson received it, May 8, 1833, he needed to cross to the west side of White River. He asked Michael van Blaricum, the ferryman at Washington Street, to row him across.

McPherson evidently was unaware that Van Blaricum hated him, disliking McPherson's reputation as a dude and the fact his wife liked McPherson. Van Blaricum had sworn to drown McPherson if he got the chance. He got his opportunity that day.

In the ten-foot water of midstream, Van Blaricum stood and rocked the boat until it upset and then swam toward shore. McPherson was unable to swim, although it is unknown if the ferryman knew that. The timekeeper clung to the capsized boat and called for help. Van Blaricum swam back, and the two began struggling in the water.

McPherson sank and drowned. When the body was retrieved, doctors said that there were finger marks around McPherson's throat.

Van Blaricum was charged with murder. At his trial, there was considerable debate over whether the roughhousing in the water was intended to kill McPherson or merely frighten him. But Van Blaricum had been accused of "willfully upsetting the boat." He was convicted only of manslaughter and sentenced to four years in prison. He was pardoned on February 9, 1835, by Governor Noah Noble.

What happened to Mary Barbee and how she overcame the sadness of a lost love seem buried in history.

# Holmes and Homicides

One of the most sensational serial murder cases of the 1890s came to a head in Indianapolis after the slayer spent considerable time with crime in Chicago. The killer not only counted twenty-seven victims in an article he wrote before he was hanged in Philadelphia, his twisted career of torture and death was also part of a 2003 volume, *The Devil in the White City*. That nonfiction work interwove the castle built on Chicago's south side by the killer, with the construction and opening of the World's Columbian Exposition in Chicago in 1893.

The castle at which Herman W. Mudgett, alias H.H. Holmes, began his dizzying scheme of insurance fraud and murder was located at Wallace and Sixty-second Street in Chicago, near the flamboyant Columbian Exposition. The exposition, in fact, may have provided a coverup for the intricate castle; many assumed the building was being remodeled into a hostelry for the expected exposition crowds. But it was full of trapdoors, passages and hidden rooms, including a gas chamber, used for mass murder.

Suspicions grew in Chicago, and Holmes left, staying briefly in Irvington in Indianapolis. He committed only one known murder in Indianapolis, but it was part of his downfall, thanks to tireless work by Philadelphia detective Frank P. Geyer.

Holmes, who called himself a doctor, seemed to attract women, despite what some considered a sinister look in his eyes. Born in New Hampshire, he was handsome, with an Oriental cast to his face, and wore a thick mustache.

People began entering the Holmes Castle, never to be heard from again. Emaline C. Cigand disappeared a few weeks after being hired as Holmes's secretary. Emily van Tassel followed. She was seen around the castle for a few weeks and then vanished. Holmes had married Myrta Z. Belknap in 1887, although he had neglected to mention a previous wife, Clara Lovering.

Despite his confusing marital status, Holmes proposed to Minnie Williams of Fort Worth, Texas, who wrote to her sister, Nannie, to come to Chicago for the wedding. Both women disappeared. They had signed over Texas property worth $50,000 to Holmes. Suspicious relatives wrote to him. But Holmes gave believable excuses—they were visiting friends, they had gone on trips and so on.

Emboldened, Holmes embarked on a dangerous course—he took on an accomplice, Benjamin F. Pitezel of Philadelphia, Pennsylvania. Pitezel would take out a $10,000 insurance policy and then vanish. Holmes would procure a body to be later identified as Pitezel. They would split the $10,000 insurance. But Pitezel died in an "accidental" explosion. Holmes convinced Pitezel's widow, Carrie, that her husband was in hiding for a while. Holmes talked her out of the insurance money. He also took the three Pitezel children under his wing, ostensibly to relieve the ill Carrie of their care.

Tenacious Geyer investigated Pitezel's disappearance. Holmes, under questioning, disclaimed any knowledge of Pitezel's disappearance or of the Pitezel children—Alice, fifteen; Nellie, thirteen; and Howard, ten. But he was held in Moyamensing Prison in Philadelphia under suspicion in the Benjamin Pitezel case.

Chicago investigators found an "operating room" that contained a butcher's table. In a big stove in the basement of the now empty castle were found bleached bones, a watch chain and a garter buckle that had belonged to Minnie and Nannie Williams.

Geyer armed himself with photos of the missing Pitezel children and began searching Chicago, Cincinnati and Detroit without luck. But a search in a house in which Holmes had lived in Toronto, Canada, produced decomposed bodies identified as the two Pitezel girls. They were found buried in the earthen basement.

Newspapers recounted the H.H. Holmes case and showed some of his victims. Indianapolis Star *files*.

Geyer came to Indianapolis, perhaps having learned that Holmes had spent some time in the Hoosier capital. His canvass of realty offices brought him to a real estate man named Brown in east-side Irvington. Brown remembered Holmes, who had rented a small cottage in October 1894. Numerous people recalled Holmes and a little boy. At the Shank grocery store, they remembered him buying milk, although the amount of milk purchased kept diminishing.

While searching the now vacant cottage, Geyer saw something blue through a crack in the floor. It was part of an old trunk on which was a piece of blue calico with a flower. Carrie Pitezel confirmed that her son Howard had possessed such a trunk.

Three neighborhood boys began poking around the empty cottage. They discovered teeth and bits of bone in the base of the chimney. The exploring detective found charred human remains; they were identified as those of Howard Pitezel.

The Irvington home that Holmes rented and that contained clues to his murders still exists. *Photo by author.*

On September 12, 1895, a Philadelphia grand jury indicted Holmes for the murder of Benjamin Pitezel. In Toronto, Holmes was indicted for the murder of the two Pitezel girls. In Indianapolis, Holmes was indicted for the murder of Howard Pitezel. Holmes was convicted in Philadelphia and sentenced to hang.

Meanwhile, the Holmes Castle in Chicago had burned to the ground. Arson, to cover up the details of the mansion of murder, was suspected. No one was ever arrested.

Holmes wrote his memoirs, beginning in December 1864 while he was in the Philadelphia prison. Some of it was fabricated. It included a "diary" of his daily life in prison. According to most reports, he got $5,000 from a newspaper for this account of his activities.

Although he revealed a lot, Holmes did not tell all. "In conclusion," he wrote, "I wish to say that I am but a very ordinary man, even below average in physical strength and mental ability, and to have planned and executed the stupendous amount of wrong-doing that has been attributed to me would have been wholly beyond my power."

Reported the *Chicago Times-Herald*: "He [Holmes] is a prodigy of wickedness, a human demon, a being so unthinkable that no novelist would dare to invent such a character."

Herman W. Mudgett, alias Dr. H.H. Holmes, was hanged on May 7, 1896. Some said that he was as nonchalant walking to the gallows as he had been in life—duping insurance companies and committing a string of murders seemingly as long as the rope around his neck.

# Murder for Profit

Money was evidently the motive in the slaying of a man and his wife outside the northwest Indianapolis boundaries on a September Saturday afternoon in 1868. The double homicide was enough to set the city agog, but it also revealed a series of startling mysteries still unresolved.

The female mastermind of the murders, and who probably fired one of the fatal shots, survived five trials. Perjury finally put her behind bars. The intriguing trials of Nancy Clem were conducted in part by Benjamin Harrison, later to become president of the United States. They may have been Harrison's first public recognition.

The victims were Jacob Young and his wife, Nancy Jane. The site was at Cold Spring, about four miles northwest of White River, then outside the city limits. Young had been felled by a shotgun blast, and his wife, whose body was found some distance away, had a pistol wound in the back of her head. Nancy Jane's body had been burned from the knees to the face. The shotgun was found on a sandbar about ten feet from Jacob Young's body.

A buggy was found tied to a nearby pawpaw tree. Hoof marks, buggy ruts and an imprint of a woman's shoe were about the only other clues. The shotgun was traced to pawnbroker Joseph Solomon, who had sold it for ten dollars to William J. Abrams, a carpenter.

Soon, Mrs. Clem's brother, Silas (Syke) Hartman, was arrested. Nine days after the murders, Mrs. Clem was also seized on a murder charge. Also charged was Abrams, who also was a business associate of Young's. The entanglements began expanding.

First was the mystery of Jacob Young himself. He had been in Indianapolis only five years, arriving poor and getting a job as a hardware store porter. Somehow, Young started handling large sums of money, boldly showing pockets full of bills wrapped in newspapers.

Mrs. Clem had been married to William Patton. When he died, she married William F. Clem, son of a well-known grocer. Mrs. Clem lived next door to another brother, Matthew Hartman.

Mrs. Clem—quiet, fond of gardening, illiterate and able to write only her name—was described as "distractingly pretty," money-mad and evidently capable of complex monetary manipulations. She borrowed at exorbitant interest rates and repaid them in a matter of days.

It was suspected that Mrs. Clem was repaying loans with newly borrowed loans and maybe intended to make a large final loan and leave town. However, none of this came to light until after the murders.

Whether Young and his wife were involved in Mrs. Clem's money scams is unclear, but they were good friends. Young also had some connection with a Clem obligation that was coming due on the twelfth of the month. On Friday, Young had shown a banker about $6,000 in one of his newspaper packages. He had changed two $500 bills for smaller bills.

The next afternoon, the Youngs went riding in a buggy. The next day, September 13, a swimmer found their bodies. Young's pocketbook, lying on the ground near his body, contained just twelve dollars.

When Mrs. Clem was arrested, she was wearing the shoes of a servant girl, similar to the footprints found at the murder site.

At trial, the defense was led by William P. Fishback, one of Ben Harrison's partners. Harrison did not take part in this first trial. He was busy as an Indiana Supreme Court reporter.

Witnesses placed Mrs. Clem in the buggy with the Youngs and her brother, Silas, behind in another carriage, drawn by his mare, Pet. Mrs. Clem's financial transactions were exhibited, but they yielded little clarity. In the end, one juror held out for acquittal. Mrs. Clem was remanded for a new trial.

It began in February 1869, four months after the murder. This time, Harrison, who had left his job with the Supreme Court, took part for the prosecution. Again the evidence of the shoe print and the horseshoe print was given. It was shown that Mrs. Clem had returned home with her brother, Silas.

On the day Abrams had been arrested, it was shown that Mrs. Clem had hidden a large roll of money in an empty peach can in her sister-in-law's cellar, saying that she feared her home would be searched. A day later,

Benjamin Harrison gained recognition for prosecuting the Nancy Clem trial and later became president of the United States.

Abrams sent a messenger to Mrs. Clem, and he was given between $4,000 and $5,000.

Harrison produced a witness, a neighbor of Mrs. Clem's, who testified that Mrs. Clem and her brother had returned home the evening of September 12 and that Mrs. Clem had bribed him to leave Indianapolis during the first trial. Harrison also presented new evidence of Mrs. Clem's complicated money dealings and brought out that Young was Mrs. Clem's largest creditor.

Mrs. Clem was found guilty of second-degree murder and sentenced to life in prison.

Within a few days, her brother Silas confessed that he had done the killing and that Mrs. Clem was innocent. This ploy seemingly was to keep him from a death sentence and lessen Mrs. Clem's imprisonment. Back in jail, Silas Hartman talked in private to Mrs. Clem in an adjoining cell after Abrams hung a blanket to shield their conversation. The next morning, Hartman had fatally cut his throat with a razor loaned to the prisoner to shave himself.

Abrams was tried, convicted and, like Mrs. Clem, sentenced to life imprisonment. He was pardoned on July 3, 1878, by Governor James D. "Blue Jeans" Williams.

The Indiana Supreme Court reviewed Mrs. Clem's case and ordered a new trial, based on incorrect jury instructions. The third trial was held in Boone County; again Harrison participated. Again Mrs. Clem was convicted. Again the Supreme Court ordered a new trial, citing bad instructions to the jury.

The fourth and fifth trials were also held in Lebanon. Both resulted in convictions. Again the Supreme Court found errors in each trial and called for a sixth trial. The Marion County commissioners, however, declined to pay for further prosecution. Mrs. Clem was released.

Audaciously, she began her loan racket again, but she was stopped by charges of obtaining money under false pretenses. At trial, she was acquitted of the swindling but convicted of perjury. She served four years in the woman's prison. Her long-suffering husband divorced her, and she came out of prison friendless—except, amazingly, for her first husband, William Patton.

For a time, she peddled patent medicine for Michael Slavin, who considered her one of his best salesmen. She earned fifty to sixty dollars per week.

On June 8, 1897, at age sixty-five, ill with Bright's disease and stomach cancer, Nancy Clem died at 11:00 p.m. at Slavin's home. Reporters hovered as Mrs. Clem drew her last breaths, hoping for deathbed confessions. But she died without ever admitting that she had killed the Youngs and without ever revealing anything about her earlier loan schemes. There were only deliriums.

# The Sugar Bowl Slaying

It was a killing in the heat of the moment that evening in 1917, but it took on racial overtones in an era of considerable prejudice between whites and African Americans in Indianapolis and elsewhere. It started over a discussion about sugar in a downtown Indianapolis café. Many considered the outcome of the case a reflection of the unfairness to blacks in the era, but even so, a white man was actually indicted and tried for killing an African American. The outcome, after a fairly long trial, left both whites and blacks dissatisfied, with newspapers either deriding or applauding the verdict. An overlaying issue also was alcohol use, which in that period was coming under criticism, later to culminate in Prohibition. Despite the World War I news splattering across the pages of Indianapolis newspapers, the slaying of Clarence Euell, a waiter, by Dan Shay, an out-of-town minor league baseball team manager, was given prominent coverage.

It was the evening of May 3 when Shay, fresh from his Milwaukee Brewers defeat (3–1) by the Indianapolis Indians, entered the café of the English Hotel. It was an elegant hostelry built shortly after the Civil War on the city's centerpiece, Monument Circle, and it was the place to go. The hotel contained an opera house that hosted many national celebrities and was large enough to have staged *Ben-Hur*, chariots and all.

Shay was staying there. A native of Springfield, Ohio, the forty-one-year-old Shay had started playing baseball in the minors in 1895 and then played in the Major Leagues in seven cities before a finger injury hampered his already weak hitting; he was released by the New York Giants. After two years back in the minors, he got some management jobs.

The Claypool was not Shay's first postgame stop. He got drinks at the Indy tavern of a friend and then had spent two hours with a "manicurist," revealed to have done more than nails for customers. He and the manicurist arrived at the Claypool café about 8:30 p.m. Drinks were ordered, plus steak, potatoes and salad.

Euell was the waiter. At dispute were details of what happened next. Only three people knew precisely. One was Euell, the deceased. The other two were Shay and his manicurist companion, thirty-six-year-old Gertrude Anderson, and their stories changed considerably during the ensuing days.

What was undisputed is that Shay asked for additional sugar for his post-meal coffee, and Euell pointed out there already was sugar on the table. Shay rose, pulled out a pistol—he owned and carried a gun—and fired a shot into Euell's belly. Anderson and Elizabeth Braskett, the white cashier (she had heard little of what transpired), fled through the kitchen. Herbert

In the English Hotel, Clarence Euell was shot to death. The café was located in the right corner. *Library of Congress.*

Miller, the manager, heard the shot and came running. He found Shay and Euell grappling on the floor. The waiter had seized Shay's wrist before he could fire another shot, threw him down, pinned his head against the floor and was pounding it as Miller entered. When admonished, Euell objected that he had been shot and claimed that he had a right to pound the assailant.

Another black waiter, Mark Byrd, handed Miller the dropped gun. Miller put it in the safe and later gave it to police. The manager called police and an ambulance, while Euell waited in the kitchen. Then the waiter painfully asked Miller to send "me someplace to die" and was told to sit in the hotel lobby. Some of Shay's baseball players, who had been in the lobby, rushed Shay to his room upstairs.

Arriving police sent Euell to the hospital and seized Shay and booked him for assault. Police planned to take Shay to City Hospital so that Euell could identify him when they learned that the waiter had died. Shay was charged with second-degree murder and denied bond, and the convoluted testimony of the participants began. Testimony given to police, before the grand jury, in the newspapers and in court quickly turned a seemingly open-and-shut case of homicide into a more complex drama.

Shay lost his job as baseball manager. The baseball world collected a defense fund for Shay, and he obtained a powerful local law firm. The two black newspapers in Indianapolis, the *Freeman* and the *Colored World*, provided few details about Euell's death, except to say he had been shot and reportedly had a good reputation. There was business to be considered; the cautious owner of the *Freeman* operated a barbershop that catered to mostly whites. It appeared that African Americans, upset over the shooting, feared it might not be vigorously prosecuted and raised money to push the case.

Shay and Anderson, who could not be located for two days, gave similar stories; although Shay had said that Anderson would corroborate his version, she gave two conflicting accounts. The resulting trial, which began November 14, sifted down to this scenario: the prosecution contended that Shay had been drinking, was disorderly and lacked the motive to shoot Euell. The defense claimed that Euell had been slow and surly, had clenched his fist and threatened Shay so that he feared for his safety. Shay even claimed that Euell had struck him in the face with the sugar bowl.

The jury started considering the case at 11:00 p.m. on November 21. At 9:00 a.m. the next day, the members of the jury returned the verdict. The acquittal came as little surprise; there was applause in the courtroom. Shay had been confident of the outcome. "I felt any fair-minded man would look at the case in the same light the jury did," Shay said. The African American newspapers deplored the verdict, as did at least one of the city's dailies. One editorial said that even if Euell had been inattentive and a bit lecherous (he had been accused of "leering" at Anderson), "the penalty for these affronts is not death."

Shay did some baseball scouting—his management days were over—and moved to Kansas City, where he got a clerking job at city hall. He digressed into alcoholism and shot himself in December 1927 in the Kansas City Majestic Hotel. It is not recorded if it occurred in the hotel café.

# The Last Hanging

There was no doubt that George Barrett had committed murder. But what followed it was one of the most bizarre spectacles of another era in Indianapolis history. The hanging of Barrett was attended by an estimated five thousand people in the Marion County Jail courtyard. It also had the ghoulish ambiance of a former circus trapeze artist springing the trap, a female spectator fainting and another onlooker vomiting. One of the calmest of all was Barrett, who went to the gallows with his previously confiscated glass eye properly affixed. It had been seized lest he pulverize it and commit suicide by swallowing the pieces.

The slaying Barrett committed was an Indiana crime by a mere twenty-two feet. On August 14, 1935, FBI agents, suspecting Barrett in an interstate auto theft ring, traced him to College Corners. The town straddles the Indiana-Ohio state line, with Union County on the Hoosier side.

FBI agents from Cincinnati staked out Barrett's stolen car, but Barrett had been warned. He approached the vehicle carrying a rolled-up towel. When the agents called for Barrett to halt, he fled up an alley. Agent Nelson B. Klein ran in pursuit up the alley and was mortally wounded. Nearby was the towel Barrett had been carrying. Inside was a .45-caliber Colt, its clip empty. Klein was the first federal agent killed in a gunfight in Indiana. He suffered five gunshot wounds. Barrett fled into the woods, where he was captured, wounded in the leg.

Since the slaying, a federal case, had taken place in Indiana, the trial was moved to a federal court in Indianapolis. It started on December 2. The sentence, at the time, was hanging for killing a federal agent.

Although Barrett looked like a Bible salesman, this tall Kentuckian had a long rap sheet. As a teenager, he had been jailed in 1913 for moonshining; the altercation cost him an eye. In 1931, he was tried twice for murdering his mother and sister; both trials resulted in hung juries. In 1933, Barrett was accused of killing Frank Baker, the prosecutor in the earlier murder trials. Again Barrett escaped via a hung jury.

Barrett attended his Indianapolis trial in a wheelchair because of his wounded leg. Despite the obvious outcome, the jury pondered nearly two days. It was said that they prolonged deliberations to get a few more free meals. When Barrett was found guilty, a U.S. marshal impounded his glass eye.

Judge Robert Baltzell, new to the federal bench, ordered Barrett to be hanged in the Marion County Jail courtyard, then located on South Alabama Street. Fearing a circus atmosphere, the judge ordered a tent built to shield the jailhouse gallows. A hangman called in from Illinois delightedly held a press conference to recount his qualifications and demonstrate the hangman's knot. The Barrett hanging would be the last to occur in Marion County.

It was set for one minute after midnight on Tuesday, March 24, 1936. Although only government officials and the press were authorized to watch the execution, thousands asked the court to attend. On Monday afternoon before the hanging, five thousand men, women and children jammed Alabama Street, blocking traffic. It was agreed that if they went single file, they could view the gallows.

The fateful day, Barrett ordered steak and took his glass eye out of the bathrobe he was wearing. "The sheriff gave it back to me for this occasion," he told the press. Suddenly, it was learned that the hangman from Illinois would put the black hood over Barrett's head, make the knot and loop the rope around his neck but not spring the trapdoor. Someone else would have to do that, he said; it wasn't part of the job.

Sheriff Otto Ray called a meeting of deputies and asked for a volunteer. After some delay, Charley Reeves stepped forward. Reeves, at five feet tall, was a midget beside Barrett. Reeves had once performed on the circus trapeze. He was whisked away to be given instructions. People with "influence" found their way into the jail courtyard, although they were barred from the hanging tent. In it, about forty witnesses occupied wooden chairs.

At 11:50 p.m., Barrett, in his new black suit, was carried out of the jail on a stretcher—his leg wound was still unhealed. The procession included a newspaperman carrying two candles, a priest and four robust deputies. A woman in the crowd fainted. The procession continued, stepping deftly over her body. As Barrett was hauled up the traditional thirteen steps, someone among the witnesses vomited, the gagging providing a macabre irony in the tent. The hangman, who didn't do the hanging, performed his part of the task, and at 12:01 a.m., ex-circus performer Charley Reeves, with a hefty swing, severed the rope holding the gallows doors, and Barrett paid for his murder.

It was the first execution in Marion County since 1886 and the last hanging in the county's history.

# Claypool Corpses

The Claypool Hotel, long a centerpiece in downtown Indianapolis in addition to being the site of many dramatic civic events, was also the scene of not one but two murders, slightly more than a decade apart. The hotel, built in 1903 at Washington and Illinois Streets near the statehouse, was located in the heart of downtown and was long the jousting headquarters of both political parties. It is gone now, but the echo of violence in those bygone rooms lingers. One of the murders was solved with an arrest within a few months. The other slaying, the first in the Claypool, still begs for a solution.

It began on a Saturday afternoon in August 1943 when a thirty-two-year-old WAC arrived from Camp Atterbury, south of Indianapolis, on a weekend pass. Corporal Maoma Little Ridings had stayed at the hotel several times, occasionally with other WACs. This time, she was shown alone to room 729; except for a bellboy and the murderer, Corporal Ridings was never seen alive again.

Ridings, capable and well liked at Atterbury, was a divorced physiotherapist who once had served President Franklin D. Roosevelt in that capacity. Roosevelt had been her patient at the hospital of Warm Springs (Georgia) Infantile Paralysis Foundation. At the time, Ridings was employed by the Federal Housing Administration in Washington, D.C., and was living in Virginia. She was divorced from Lawrence Ridings, who was serving overseas with the army.

Ridings entered the army, took training at Daytona Beach, Florida, and was assigned to Camp Atterbury on March 6, 1943. At first she was a member of the 44th Women's Army Auxiliary Corps Company but later was transferred to the Women's Army Corps assigned to headquarters company of the 3561st WAC service unit and given duty as a physiotherapist at the Atterbury base hospital.

On the day of her murder, Ridings left the camp on the 3:30 p.m. bus on August 28, armed with a pass good until Monday morning. By 5:00 p.m., she was registering at the hotel, not far from the Indianapolis bus depot. About thirty minutes later, bellboy Alfred Bayne Jr. delivered six bottles of soft drinks and ice to Ridings's room. She seemed in good spirits and tipped him. Bayne noticed a woman in black sitting on the bed—black hat, black frock, black veil, attractive (as much as could be seen) and thirty-five to forty years old. Less than an hour later, more ice was ordered; bellboy Robert Wolfington made the delivery. A feminine voice from the bathroom told Wolfington to leave the ice and take the quarter left on the dresser for him.

**Hotel History**

MAOMA RIDINGS          DOROTHY POORE

Newspapers found photos of the two women killed at the Claypool Hotel. Indianapolis Star *files*.

The old Claypool Hotel hosted many political activities, such as this in 1952, but it was also the site of two murders. Indianapolis Star *files*.

About three hours later, Mrs. Lillian McNamara, a hotel housekeeper, went to Ridings's room to "clean up." Supposedly, the occupants had checked out. Another version was that McNamara was making a routine room inspection. However, the hall door to room 729 was blocked. When she forced it, she was able to see that a woman was lying between the bed and the door, arms stretched backward above the head and nude from the waist down.

"It was a ghastly sight," Mrs. McNamara told police. "There was a large pool of blood a foot from her head. Her face was almost drowned in blood, and there were deep, jagged cuts in her neck, her arms and her wrists. One cut in the left side of her neck appeared to be about four inches long and very deep."

McNamara called the switchboard operator, who called police. The only article in the room that might have made cuts in Ridings was a broken whiskey bottle, but there was no blood on it. The room was splattered with blood, but there was no indication of a struggle. A quarter lay in the blood by the victim's head.

The bed, unruffled, had a corner of the sheet turned back. The corporal's underwear and a cape were atop the bed in a neat pile. While police were there, a detective answered the phone to hear a man's voice ask if Miss Ridings was there. He refused to give his name and, when told she was not there, said, "Thanks very much" and hung up.

Investigation by deputy coroner Dr. E.H. Hare revealed that the crime had been made to look like suicide; cuts in her wrists were superficial. The body, taken to Fort Benjamin Harrison for the autopsy, revealed that Ridings had been killed elsewhere in the room and dragged to the door. "It appears that the woman's wrists had been slashed after she was struck on the head and cut in the neck, possibly after her heart had stopped beating," said Coroner Roy B. Storms. "There was only a slight flow of blood from the slashes on her wrists." Death had come from a severed jugular vein, although she had suffered a hard blow to the head. "There is a good probability that Corporal Ridings was criminally assaulted before she was murdered," said Storms. The body of Ridings was released to relatives at Warm Springs, Georgia.

Police had a lot to work with, but little panned out. Wolfington was grilled for several days but was released. The mystery of the phone call was cleared up. Corporal Emanuel Fisher of Camp Atterbury said that he had called because he had a date with Ridings. When a man answered, he had hung up. But the woman in black was never identified. Bayne said that the woman kept silent while he was in the room, "but she appeared to be in good humor." Some suggested that it might have been a female impersonator. "She looked pretty feminine to me," said Bayne.

Jack Manaheim, who was next to room 729, told police that he had been there all evening but had heard nothing unusual and certainly no struggle. Richard Fearand, eighteen and from New Castle, had bragged to friends that he had stayed in an Indianapolis hotel the night Ridings died and knew "a lot about the killing." Police doubted that he had anything to do with the murder but held him for awhile anyhow. A WAC's skirt, about Ridings's size, was found in the 1900 block of North Tibbs Avenue by milk wagon driver Francis Sigeman. Nothing came of it or of a report that a bloody skirt was taken to a dry cleaners on Illinois Street. WACs were questioned at Camp Atterbury. Investigators learned nothing except that Ridings was well liked and had a spotless military record. The coroner backed off his speculation that Ridings had been sexually assaulted.

Some wild speculations, such as jealousy and that the "woman in black" had been a foreign agent, were discarded by police. Nobody ever learned why the WAC from Georgia had been murdered in an Indianapolis hotel room at the start of a weekend of fun in the "big city."

# Room 665

As with Corporal Ridings, the body of Dorothy Poore was discovered by Claypool housekeepers on a hot day in July 1954. The eighteen-year-old victim was stuffed in a dresser drawer. From that moment, the homicide became known as the "dresser drawer murder case." Although the murderer of Ridings was never found, Dorothy's killer was discovered and arrested rather quickly.

Dorothy's body was badly decomposed, posing problems for the coroner. But it was determined that she had been strangled or had suffocated before being forced into the dresser in room 665. Authorities speculated that it might have taken two persons to perform that difficult task. It was estimated that Dorothy, whose full name turned out to be Lillian Dorothy Poore, had been dead about thirty-six hours. The stench forced the hotel to evacuate the entire sixth floor.

Police almost immediately focused on a sadistic sex fiend as the possible killer. A pair of sandals, a pair of blue jeans, a white shirtwaist and a broken blue plastic belt were found stuffed in an air space in the hotel room closet. Fingerprints were found. A Buick automobile parked in the garage used by the hotel was possibly related to the crime, police said. They also wanted to find a man who gave the name of John O'Brien and had rented the room the previous Thursday. He had said he was a salesman from New York City.

O'Brien was described as well dressed, in his middle thirties and of medium build, with a smooth, light complexion. Hotel personnel who had seen him said that he resembled Van Johnson, a popular screen actor of that era. At one point, housekeepers had seen O'Brien seated on the bed, explaining that a spot of blood on the sheets was from a nosebleed resulting from a sinus condition. He had paid for the room until Saturday's checkout time but never checked out. No one entered the room until about 10:00 a.m. on Sunday, when the murder was discovered.

Dorothy, about five feet, six inches tall, with dark hair, was the daughter of Mrs. Hazel Poore, a waitress divorcée who lived in the Clinton, Indiana suburb of Fair View. Dorothy had come to Indianapolis on her third trip there to try to obtain a job. Dorothy had spent most of her life in Clinton in Vermillion County after being born in Chicago. She was a 1953 graduate of Clinton High School. She had checked into the Lorraine Hotel, a short distance from the Claypool, on Saturday and had hoped to take a Civil Service examination five days after her body was found. She had first come to Indianapolis on July 1, staying two nights in the Lorraine and spending some time with a former classmate who was working in Indianapolis and staying with relatives.

On trips back to Clinton, Dorothy told her grandmother, her closest confidante, that men on the street had followed her twice. One, she said, took her travel bag and examined it in the bus station before returning it, and the other said that he was a bus terminal detective assigned to protect young girls. Perhaps taking that as a premonition, Dorothy's mother accompanied her on July 8 on her job search in Indianapolis. After a couple of days, Dorothy, at her mother's behest, returned home. On Wednesday, July 14, the girl made her third—and last—job-hunting trip.

The two housekeepers noticed the smell when they entered the room and called for William M. Kimbrough, the house boy, who opened the drawer. Investigators found a blue cloth handbag behind a radiator. It was Dorothy's and contained a blank social security application, an address book, a package of chewing gum and five cents in change. Soon, police found the clothing where water pipes and an air vent came into the room through the closet.

Police began to hunt for O'Brien. Since they suspected a phony name, they asked hotel personnel to come up with a drawing of the man they had seen. Later, at the urging of an Indianapolis reporter, police began canvassing other hotels in the area. In one they found the name of Victor Lively in handwriting matching that used by O'Brien. A check revealed that Lively had worked at an Indianapolis laundry and had driven a taxi and gave his home as Beaumont, Texas. Lively's fingerprints matched those found in the murder room.

A police bulletin resulted in the apprehension of Lively at Clayton, Missouri, on July 23, five days after the discovery of Poore's body. Lively had been picked up while hitchhiking en route to Texas. Within hours, he admitted killing Dorothy. Indianapolis homicide detectives took Bruno Widmann, a bellhop at the Claypool, to Missouri to identify Lively, but it proved needless. Lively readily admitted seeing Widmann at the Claypool.

Lively told Missouri authorities that he had asked a cab driver about girls he might date. The cabbie said that he knew one but that she would not go out without her friend. Rejecting that idea, Lively said that he returned to his Claypool room to write a letter to his ex-wife. About midnight, he said, two girls named Ruth and Dorothy came to his room. "Ruth" never was fully identified, but after about two and a half hours of talking about jobs, she and Dorothy had an argument and Ruth left. Dorothy stayed, Lively related.

Lively claimed that he was drinking gin and water, but "Dot," as he called her, wanted whiskey, which he refused to get because it was late and obtaining it from the bellboy would have been expensive. Dot, he said, became angry and began slapping him. He tried to restrain her; "I don't know what happened," he said. Lively said he thought he put his hands around her throat. "I thought she was dead," he said.

It was about 2:30 a.m. on July 16, Lively said, and he sat for hours drinking the rest of the gin. There was nobody in the room except him and the corpse, he said. When it got daylight, Lively put Dot, who was wearing a slip, bra and pants, into the dresser drawer. Then he stuffed jeans, shoes and a blouse in the air tunnel in the closet. Dot had taken them off the night before, Lively claimed. Having done that, Lively said he left the hotel about 9:30 a.m. and went to East St. Louis, Illinois, and called his boss. On Saturday night, broke, he slept in the bus depot in East St. Louis.

Lively was returned to Indianapolis, tried and convicted of the murder on December 2, 1954. He was sentenced to life.

# Part III

# CATALOGUE OF SLAUGHTER

## Murder for $1.20

Pharmacist William H. Bright was going home for supper that evening in January 1937. He had just left the drugstore where he worked on East Tenth Street near downtown Indianapolis. When he halted his car for a stoplight, two young men leaped in and forced him to drive to northwest Shelby County, at least ten miles from that stoplight.

There the pair walked him into a cornfield. Probably because Bright carried only $1.20, the would-be robbers shot him to death and tossed his body over the nearby bridge at Big Sugar Creek near the Red Mill, a landmark that survives.

Little data about Bright survives. But soon after that January 4, he was reported missing. A search was begun, and on January 6, blood on the bridge railing prompted a search of the creek. In twelve feet of water, much more than the creek contains now, his body was found, riddled with four bullets. His hat, containing bullet holes, was found later.

This slaying might have gone unsolved had not an automobile heater been sold to a man in Madison. It had come from Bright's car. With that as a lead, Vurtis Neal was soon captured in Carroll County, Kentucky. He was placed under arrest by his Uncle Jake, who was an Indiana state policeman. Hugh Marshall Jr. was picked up in Indianapolis. Neal was twenty-two and Marshall was nineteen.

Soon, details of the crime emerged. The pair had visited Marshall's father, Hugh Sr., and told him of their plans to stop a car, steal the vehicle and rob its passenger. The senior Marshall gave them advice and encouragement, police said. And so the two young men stood by a stoplight, waiting for a patsy.

Why they drove to Shelby County is anybody's guess, except for the obvious possibility that they feared that the presence of Indianapolis policemen made robbing Bright dangerous in the city. However, just after they forced Bright to walk in the cornfield, Marshall handed the gun to Neal, and then he found that Bright carried only $1.20. Bright was doomed.

A Shelby County grand jury indicted the pair for murder and murder in the commission of a robbery, a charge that carried a mandatory term of death. Both youths pleaded not guilty, which Marshall soon changed to an insanity plea; Neal followed suit. A death penalty trial was unusual in Shelbyville. It took five days and the summoning of 123 jurors before a panel of 11 farmers and 1 railroad man was chosen. The trial began on March 23.

About 11:00 p.m., on April 5, a guilty verdict was returned. The defense had tried to show that Marshall was not responsible for his actions. They pointed to his time in a home for the feebleminded at Fort Wayne. They

The Red Mill still stands; near it an Indianapolis pharmacist was slain for $1.20. *Photo by author.*

also suggested that the robbery charge was incorrect because the pair had commandeered the car in another county. The jury was unconvinced. It deliberated for about three hours. Twenty minutes after the verdict, the two were sentenced to death.

At 12:07 a.m., on July 8, Marshall was led to the electric chair in the prison at Michigan City. He was dead five minutes later. Neal followed, and by 12:20 a.m., he paid with his life as well. Neither had made a comment.

One side note to the sensational trial was the arrest of Hugh Marshall Sr. as an accessory before and after the murder, based in his failure to try to deter the youths from their robbery aim. By November, however, the charges were dropped, and Marshall was freed.

Today, only the empty Red Mill, the creek that meanders near it and the few who may recall druggist Bright survive as echoes of that fatal 1937 moment in a Shelby County cornfield.

# Murder after Twelve Days

The death of Madge Oberholtzer, if it be murder (some doubt it), is odd for several reasons. First, it is one of the few times that the victim had the time and the opportunity to give the details of the crime. Second, it involved a prominent citizen, D.C. Stephenson, who considered himself "the law" in Indiana and had lived an immoral lifestyle alien to the tenets of his organization, the Ku Klux Klan. Thirdly, the death of Oberholtzer eventually helped bring down the Klan, which before her death had a growing political hold on an entire state.

By 1924, David Curtis Stephenson, a Texan who organized and became the grand dragon of the Indiana Ku Klux Klan, had spearheaded the election of the Indiana governor and most of the officials of Indianapolis, site of D.C.'s headquarters. Although the Klan preached morality, virtue and protection of women, Stephenson, buoyed by his dictatorial power, held orgies in his east-side Indianapolis mansion and was believed to be an alcoholic and a seducer of women. He had been charged with seduction in 1924 but paid off the accuser. His rise to political power came by well-documented bribery, either monetary or political.

It is no wonder that he was a prominent figure at the festivities in late 1924 for the soon-to-be Indiana governor Ed Jackson, whose election Stephenson had orchestrated. By that time, Madge Oberholtzer was part of "the Statehouse" crowd, an employee in the Indiana Department of Education.

D.C. Stephenson, the Klan leader, was convicted of murder.

At twenty-eight, she was small (five feet, four inches, 140 pounds), unmarried (an engagement had been thwarted by World War I) and possibly harbored some political ambitions. She had attended Butler College in Indianapolis, plus a business school, and had taught and worked as a secretary before getting the state job. At the pre-inaugural dinner for Jackson, Madge met Stephenson. He was smitten. She was less so but was impressed by his position, lavish home, Cadillac and airplane. They had a few dates.

The romance cooled. Various reasons are offered. She lived with her parents not far from Stephenson's layout in Irvington. Less than three months after the Jackson dinner, on March 15, 1925, Madge returned home about 10:00 p.m. after a date and was told by her mother that someone had been calling from number 0492. She returned the call and Stephenson answered, telling her that he was leaving for Chicago and needed to see her on an important matter.

His bodyguard, Earl Gentry, a cigar-smoking former policeman, came to get Madge. They walked to Stephenson's house. There she discovered that he had been drinking, and she said in her later confession that three drinks were forced on her. Later, some wondered why Madge had gone to the house and why, knowing her aversion to liquor, she took three drinks. Others point out that Stephenson's known power and the presence of both Gentry and Stephenson henchman Earl Klenck, a deputy sheriff, gave Madge no alternative but to comply. From there, her life began to unravel, according to her confession, ending with her taking the only way out—death.

Before she died, though, her father George, outraged at Madge's condition, had filed assault charges against Stephenson. When Madge did die, the charge became first-degree murder. Stephenson thought that such a charge was absurd; he didn't force Madge to drink the drug that killed her. His enemies were framing him. However, medical men contended later at trial that Madge actually died of infection of the numerous bites Stephenson had inflicted on her body. She would have survived the mercury tablets she had taken, they said, especially if she had gotten medical attention.

The odyssey of Stephenson and Madge began that night after she started to become ill from the drinks she had taken. She said that she feared rejecting Stephenson's invitation to Chicago. "You cannot go home," she was told. At Union Station, where the group drove in Stephenson's car, they got a compartment on the train. Gentry got in the upper bunk. Madge, in her later declaration, said that Stephenson forced her into the lower bunk, climbed in and began assaulting her; she was weak and unsteady.

This is the still-standing Irvington mansion in which D.C. Stephenson resided in 1925. *Photo by author.*

"He chewed me all over my body, bit my neck and face, chewed my tongue, chewed my breasts until they bled, my back, my legs, my ankles and mutilated me all over my body," she said. After that, she said, she remembered nothing until the morning call from the porter, announcing Hammond. Detraining there, the group registered in two rooms at the Indiana Hotel, Stephenson and Madge as husband and wife. Stephenson agreed to let her send her mother a telegram, but he dictated its contents—that they were going up to Chicago, Oberholtzer said.

They ate breakfast in the room, and Madge had little more than coffee. Soon, a chauffeur named Shorty arrived; he had driven from Indianapolis in Stephenson's car. Stephenson, she said, made some apology—"that he was three degrees less than a brute"—and answered Oberholtzer's plea for money to buy a hat with $15.00. She did buy a hat, and with the $1.50 left over, she had Shorty drive her to a drugstore for "rouge." There, however, she bought the bichloride of mercury tablets.

Back at the hotel, she said, the men continued drinking alcohol, as they had throughout the trip. Madge said that she found a glass and took six of the mercury tablets while her captor slept. She had contemplated getting one of the guns and killing herself, but she decided to use the mercury because she thought it would be less disgraceful for her mother. The mercury made her very ill.

When Stephenson found out and discovered the blood that she had vomited into a cuspidor, he planned to put her in the hospital as his wife and have her stomach pumped, she said. She refused and also refused to be taken home. Stephenson decided to drive to Crown Point, south of Hammond, where they could get married. When she refused that, Stephenson ordered the group to pack up and head for Indianapolis.

"I don't know much about what happened after that," said Oberholtzer. "My mind was in a daze. I was in terrible agony." Stephenson said that he thought she was dying, but she said that he refused pleas for a doctor and rejected suggestions that he dump her from the car. "I heard him say also that he had been in a worse mess than this before and got out of it," she said.

Madge was taken to the loft over the Stephenson garage. She was told that she would stay there until she agreed to marry Stephenson. She recalled little else that happened until about 11:00 a.m. the next day, when Klenck took her home. Her parents, Oberholtzer said, were out looking for her, so Klenck carried her to a bed upstairs.

"I remember Stephenson had told me to tell everyone that I had been in an automobile accident, and he said, 'You must forget this, what is done

At one point, Madge Oberholtzer was kept in this garage; she was later taken to her parents' nearby residence. *Photo by author.*

has been done, I am the law and the power.'" When the Oberholtzers saw their daughter's condition, they summoned Dr. John K. Kingsbury; they had already consulted attorney Asa J. Smith. Two other witnesses were also present. Smith drafted Madge Oberholtzer's statement. "I am sure that I will not recover from this illness, and I believe that death is very near to me, and I have made all of the foregoing statements as my dying declaration and they are true," Madge swore.

Madge died on April 14 despite the doctors' ministrations and a blood transfusion given by her brother. Her father accused Stephenson, Gentry and Klenck of murder.

The trial of the trio was moved to Noblesville, north of Indianapolis. At its crux was whether Oberholtzer really had been under duress and whether she had been forced to take her own life, or if it had been her own decision, as the Stephenson defense contended. The trial lasted more than a month. The transcript took 2,247 pages. The jury convicted Stephenson of second-degree murder. Gentry and Klenck were acquitted. Stephenson was sentenced to life on November 25, 1925.

A footnote to the Stephenson case was the murder of Miss Edith Irene Dean. She was a prospective witness for the defense and, according to the rumor mill, would have given explosive testimony. But on June 3, 1925, while Stephenson was in jail, Miss Dean was murdered in Hamilton County. Her body, thrown on the railroad tracks in Noblesville, showed that she had been stomped to death. The official cause of death was listed as a ruptured spleen. No arrest in the case was ever made.

The former Klan leader expected Governor Jackson, who owed his election to Stephenson, to grant a pardon, but it never happened. Stung by this rebuff, Stephenson released information on Indiana political leaders that he had accumulated during his reign. Contents of two "black boxes" were revealed; the *Indianapolis Times* started a crusade that helped destroy the Klan. As a result of ensuing investigations, ex-governor Ed Jackson was indicted but escaped punishment because of the statute of limitations. Several Indianapolis officials were found guilty of various charges but, for the most part, paid small fines. The mayor, however, was sentenced to thirty days in jail. A former GOP state chairman was sent to prison for conspiracy. Officials in other cities were also indicted. The Klan, which once had claimed thousands of members in Indiana, was down to a few hundred members, effectively broken.

Stephenson failed in more than thirty appeals. Ultimately, he served thirty-one years. Paroled on March 23, 1956, Stephenson, now sixty-five years old, spent some time in Indianapolis. He served four months in jail after conviction of sexually assaulting a sixteen-year-old girl. He quietly moved to Jonesboro, Tennessee, where he died of a heart attack in 1966.

Some Hoosiers agreed with a statement Stephenson once made to a reporter: "I should have been put in jail for my political activities but I am not guilty of murder." Madge Oberholtzer and her parents did not agree.

# A Plethora of Possible Crimes

In this murder case, the suspect was prepared once for the electric chair before being granted a new trial. He had confessed to killing two Indianapolis women but later recanted the admission. He was questioned by police about other murders. At one of his trials, six women testified that he had raped or tried to rape them. In the end, Robert A. Watts paid with his life at Michigan City early on January 16, 1951.

Almost to the end, Watts, twenty-nine, felt that the National Association for the Advancement of Colored Persons would come to his rescue and obtain a stay of execution. The NAACP had obtained a new trial for Watts after his first conviction. An attempt at an insanity plea also was rejected. To the end, he denied guilt in the murder for which he was convicted and for the other murder to which he had once confessed.

The crime that brought the conviction was the slaying of Mrs. Mary Lois Burney some time during the evening of November 12, 1947. Her husband Herschel came home about 6:00 p.m. When he saw that the lights were off in his home on the far north side of Indianapolis, Burney, an Indianapolis food broker, got a neighbor, Paul Ross, later head of the Indianapolis Foundation, and the two entered the home together.

The body of the thirty-nine-year-old Mrs. Burney was found on a bed. She was clad in a light nightgown and a blue silk robe. Two sixteen-gauge shotgun shells and a bent butcher knife were on the floor. Police theorized that someone had entered the Burney home and tried to attack the woman; she struggled and grabbed the shotgun and it went off, blasting away most of her face.

Watts, who had been picked up for investigation in other crimes, was in police custody when Mrs. Burney's body was found. He was being questioned about the unsolved slaying of WAC corporal Maoma Ridings, who was slain in August 1943 in a Claypool Hotel room. She was killed via a severed jugular vein.

Watts had worked in hotels, investigators found, and had been on furlough from the Coast Guard at the time Ridings was killed. It was also believed that he had worked part-time at the Claypool.

Watts was also a suspect in the slaying of Mrs. Dorothy Steck, fifty, who had been beaten and raped on August 13, 1945, in her backyard in Indianapolis. A third murder for which Watts was a suspect was that of nurse Alberta Green, who was beaten to death on the morning of September 11, 1946, while in a dimly lighted corridor of the infant's ward of Rotary Convalescent Home at Riley Hospital. Police asked him about the murder of Mrs. Mabel Merrifield. She was killed in October 1947 at her Indianapolis home shortly before the Burney killing.

On November 18, Watts admitted killing Burney. Two nights later, he admitted killing Merrifield. He led investigators to a remote field, where the shotgun was found. Later, he repudiated both confessions. He contended that the admissions came after being questioned for six days and six nights, and he accused authorities of abuse during the interrogations.

In a trial that began in Shelbyville (upon a change of venue) on January 13, 1948, Watts was convicted after the jury deliberated only four hours and was sentenced to death. On February 2, he was being prepared for execution when news came that his case was being reviewed. The U.S. Supreme Court ruled that his rights had been violated because he was questioned before being formally charged.

A second trial began on March 7, 1950, at Columbus in Bartholomew County. Two factors electrified the trial. One was that Watts kept the courtroom in turmoil by shrieking at witnesses and jumping from his chair. The judge often reproached Watts for his behavior. Furthermore, six witnesses testified at the second trial that Watts had raped them or had attempted to attack them.

One was Mrs. Harriet Stout, then an executive of the Indiana League of Women Voters and wife of a department store executive. She said that Watts, driving a city truck, came to her home on November 12, 1947, and asked to use the telephone. Once inside, she testified, he grabbed a butcher knife, seized her and threatened to kill her if she did not disrobe. Stout testified at both of Watts's trials.

Investigators believed that Watts left the Stout home and proceeded only a few blocks to the Burney home. There, it was believed, he probably gained entrance with a ruse and then tried to attack Mrs. Burney.

In the second trial, the jury of eleven farmers and one industrial worker brought in a guilty verdict. Watts was again sentenced to death. The NAACP, despite Watts's conviction that it would intercede, declined to do so. Representatives from the organization said that the second trial had been fair.

Indiana governor Henry F. Schricker rejected a plea to commute the Watts death verdict to life sentence. The petitioners said that Watts had been "most if not all of his life, mentally ill."

Watts was electrocuted and pronounced dead shortly after midnight. He refused to the end to reinstate his confessions to the Burney and Merrifield murders and also resisted efforts to implicate him in other unsolved slayings.

# The Most Horrible Crime

Three times the police had been to the home on the east side of Indianapolis. They probably had little legal right to intercede, even if they had guessed that it was to become the household from hell. But there was no way of guessing. The murder committed there, called by a deputy prosecutor "the most horrible crime ever committed in the state of Indiana," was beyond normal comprehension. Even after the murder of Sylvia Likens occurred, the newspaper-reading public was stunned by the details uncovered.

# Catalogue of Slaughter

So that its horror should never be forgotten, a memorial to Sylvia Likens was erected in June 2001 in Willard Park, not far from where Sylvia met her tortured death on the evening of October 26, 1965. On her stomach had been carved "I'm a prostitute and proud of it!"—a phrase that was to echo through the community for weeks. Death came after weeks of unspeakable degradations at the hands of a thirty-seven-year-old woman with a psychopathic hatred of her brood of children and neighborhood kids drawn into the sadistic abuse.

The gang leader was Gertrude Baniszewski, who had suffered much, including poverty, but whose uncontrollable rage nevertheless seemed to have little valid source. Three of her children were directly involved, along with two neighborhood children. But there were other willing participants, guilty at least of apathy while torture proceeded in the house on East New York Street.

It started soon after the summer began, when Gertrude received an offer out of the blue: would she care for two daughters of Lester and Betty Likens for twenty dollars per week? The Likenses wanted to take their food stand barnstorming with a circus in Florida. The girls—Sylvia, sixteen, and Jenny, fifteen—moved into the Baniszewski house in July. A hitch developed almost at once. The promised twenty dollars did not show up the first week. In fact, the Likenses failed to pay or were tardy all summer. Gertrude responded to the first late payment by beating Sylvia and Jenny. It was to get horribly worse, focusing on Sylvia, a somewhat attractive blonde called "Cookie" by some. The litany of abuse Sylvia endured was almost endless. Perhaps no one but Sylvia herself ever really knew how many tortures she suffered.

This was Sylvia Likens before her torture began in Indianapolis. Indianapolis Star *files*.

The Baniszewski household existed at poverty level, getting only support money from Gertrude's ex-husband, John S. Baniszewski Sr., and occasional jobs, such as picking up cans at the Indianapolis Motor Speedway. As a result, food was short. Toast was the usual breakfast fare and soup for dinner. At one point, Sylvia got a job in the cafeteria at Tech High School, thereby obtaining a hearty lunch. But Gertrude often punished Sylvia and the others if she suspected that they had obtained food elsewhere. The house had only three spoons, so soup, heated on a hot plate, had to be eaten in shifts.

A favorite early weapon was a paddle. Gertrude used it liberally, and when she tired of it, she had her daughter Paula, seventeen, who was jealous of Sylvia, beat Sylvia with the paddle. Once, Paula broke her wrist by slugging Sylvia. She once vowed that she would beat Sylvia with the cast until it broke.

Gertrude often told lies about Sylvia, especially about her stealing and being sexually promiscuous. The other children and neighborhood children believed the lies and joined in beating Sylvia. Sometimes, Jenny was ordered to hit her sister for some transgression. Perhaps sympathy saved Jenny from abuse. She had a shriveled left leg in a steel brace, the result of polio.

Once, Sylvia and Jenny met with their older sister, Diana, and told her of the beatings in the Baniszewski household. Diana considered the information an exaggeration.

The start of school seemingly escalated the beatings. Sylvia and Stephanie Baniszewski, who was close to Sylvia's age, became fairly friendly because of their experience going to Tech together.

Police had been to the house three times, once when Baniszewski accused a neighbor of being a burglar, which proved false, again when Marie Baniszewski, eleven, fell and cut her hand and again when a newspaper boy accused Gertrude of failing to pay. On the latter run, Gertrude became violent with police. She went to court and paid one dollar and costs for failure to pay and resisting arrest. Once the public health nurse called at the home, but she filed no report. A minister visiting the home commiserated with Gertrude when she complained about her problems with Sylvia.

Gertrude had endured thirteen pregnancies and six miscarriages. She married John Baniszewski when she was sixteen, divorced him after ten years, was married in Kansas for three months to an Edward Guthrie, returned to John and divorced him again in 1963. She had lived with Dennis Lee Wright and used his name, although he had deserted her. Gertrude suffered from asthma and took phenobarbital, antihistamines and other over-the-counter drugs.

# Catalogue of Slaughter

Torturer Gertrude Baniszewski had a harried look after her arrest. Indianapolis Star *files*.

Sylvia evidently submitted to much of the torture, as if accepting fault, something similar to the battered wife syndrome. Possibly she eventually became too malnourished and weak to resist. Jenny had long since been warned to keep her mouth shut.

Sylvia urinated on one of the grungy mattresses in the house, possibly the result of some of the torture; she had been kicked in the vagina, and a Coke bottle had been inserted into it, supposedly to show what a whore Sylvia was. She was thrown into the basement since she "couldn't keep herself clean" and therefore was unfit to live upstairs. She was pronounced undeserving of food—near the end she was given soup but was required to eat it with her fingers. Feces was rubbed on her mouth; she was left only urine to drink. She slept on rags. She began receiving hot baths (since she couldn't keep clean), often with her hands and feet bound. Gertrude began putting out cigarettes on Sylvia's body, and some of the children followed suit.

Each time Sylvia was consigned to the basement, she was thrown down the stairs, which had two right angles. Coy Hubbard, fifteen and a neighbor, was shown how to throw Sylvia into the basement, which he did to improve his judo skills. He added the innovation of pinning Sylvia's arms behind her in hurling her into the basement. Now her basement cleanliness was achieved with a hosing of cold water.

That fateful Tuesday, Ricky Hobbs, fifteen, a neighbor boy, went to the Baniszewski house and found Stephanie in the basement with Sylvia. She expressed fear that the girl was dead. Hobbs noticed breathing, so Sylvia was hustled to the second floor; her body was dropped on the way. A bath was waiting. "She's faking," cried Gertrude. After the bath, done with her clothes on, Sylvia was dressed in a sweater and pedal pushers and placed on a mattress in a bedroom.

Soon, Sylvia seemed to stop breathing. Mouth-to-mouth resuscitation was tried. Accompanied by Johnny Baniszewski, Hobbs went to a Shell station across the street and called police. Patrolman Melvin D. Dixon, sent at 6:27 p.m., found a slender teenage girl on whose exposed midriff was carved "I'm a prostitute and proud of it!" plus what appeared to be the number three. Her face was covered with sores, the left side of her face wore away and open sores were around her abdomen, plus she had many bruises. Dixon knew that she was dead.

What he didn't know until later was that Gertrude Baniszewski had decided to brand Sylvia. She used a needle but soon grew tired and turned the job over to Hobbs, who heated the needle with a match to complete the job. Sylvia was too far gone to do much except groan. Hobbs found a hook in the basement and decided to heat it and have Shirley Baniszewski, ten, help him put an "S" on Sylvia. The child made a mistake, and it came out looking like a "3."

The torture slaying of young Sylvia Likens led to this Indianapolis memorial in Willard Park near the homicide site. *Photo by author.*

Gertrude told the patrolmen that Sylvia had been out with a gang of boys, who had sex with her and then inflicted the injuries. The vast number of the wounds—at least one hundred—was noted at the scene by deputy coroner Dr. Arthur Paul Kebel, who was surprised to find no evidence of sexual molestation. Pathologist Dr. Charles R. Ellis, who did the autopsy, found even more damage. Sylvia's lips were in shreds, all of her fingernails had been broken backward and her organs showed signs of malnutrition and indicated that the young victim had been in shock for perhaps two or three days. Free-flowing blood in the brain was evidence of brain pressure, a condition that brings unconsciousness and death. The shock, malnutrition and injuries were auxiliary factors to a fatal blow to the head.

Gertrude's attempt to blame the children fell through when Jenny talked at last. "You get me out of here, and I'll tell you everything," she had whispered to police that night. By midnight, Gertrude and Richard Hobbs were arrested on murder charges. Within days, other children were taken into custody on juvenile delinquency charges. By November 1965, Gertrude; her children Paula, Stephanie and Johnny; and neighbors Ricky Hobbs and Coy Hubbard had been accused of murder. They were indicted on December 30, 1965. Stephanie's case was later reconsidered by the grand jury, and she was freed.

The trial was to be as dramatic as Sylvia's short and unhappy life. Stories about the bizarre and shocking torture-murder had circulated the globe. The four attorneys representing the defendants presented Judge Saul Rabb with a blizzard of motions, including the defense of insanity and calls for psychiatric evaluations. Almost all, including those for a change of venue, were denied. Trial began on Monday, April 18, 1966. The death penalty was sought. The trial took nearly five weeks.

The verdict was guilty of first-degree murder for Gertrude Baniszewski and second-degree murder for Paula. Both were sentenced to life. Richard Hobbs, Coy Hubbard and Johnny Baniszewski were found guilty of manslaughter; their sentences were two to twenty-one years in the Indiana State Reformatory, where Johnny was the youngest ever incarcerated.

Gertrude and Paula won a reversal on appeal to the Indiana Supreme Court, which found that pretrial publicity had prejudiced the jury and that separate trials should have been granted the defendants. Gertrude was found guilty in a second trial, moved to Peru, Indiana. Paula, rather than face a retrial, pleaded guilty to manslaughter and was sentenced to two to twenty-one years in prison.

Hubbard, Hobbs and Johnny Baniszewski were paroled in 1968. Gertrude changed her name and, upon her release on parole, moved to Iowa. She died in 1990 at age sixty-two.

After the trial, Deputy Prosecutor Leroy New "adopted" Jenny, bought her a new brace and enrolled her in North Central High School some distance from Tech. She later lived in Maine and then married and lived in Beech Grove, Indiana. She attended the dedication of the memorial to Sylvia in Willard Park.

# "I Love You"——Bang, Bang, Bang

Love gone sour has been a recipe for murder for years—the stuff of movies and novels and, sometimes, in real life. It was the motive behind a 1958 homicide in Indianapolis that provided a triple dose of scandal—the status of the murder victim, the secret life behind his respectable façade and the confession and trial of his slayer. At the time, no other homicide so riveted the attention of the Indianapolis public.

Forrest Teel was the number two executive for Eli Lilly & Company, one of the premier firms in the Hoosier capital. What no one realized at first was that Teel, a married man, had been dining with the second paramour in his busy social life when he left an apartment on East Thirty-eighth Street that July 31 about 1:00 a.m. He had left behind a nineteen-year-old woman named Laura Mowrer; they had been dating for about three months. He didn't know that forty-four-year-old Conrad "Connie" Keifer Nicholas, whom he had been dating for fifteen years, was waiting in his white Cadillac with a gun and a grudge.

Of course, much of that was learned later. What was happening now was screeching brakes and the thump of a car backing against a streetlamp. In 1958, air conditioning was not prevalent and it was hot; residents with their windows open heard the commotion. Earl Alexander got out of bed to investigate. Charles Hedrick, a counterman at a nearby Howard Johnson's restaurant, joined Alexander in rushing to the automobile. The driver, slumped over the wheel, was unresponsive. Police were telephoned; there was no 911 system then, and Patrolman Richard Anderson arrived before 1:10 a.m. The man in the car said only that he wanted to go to the hospital. Lieutenant Cecil London, arriving on the scene, learned that two bullet wounds were visible. A witness identified the driver as a Lilly executive. He was sent to the hospital, but he didn't arrive there alive.

Forrest Teel was a handsome executive who courted Connie Nicholas before their love went sour. Indianapolis Star *files*.

The Indianapolis public was stunned to learn that Teel had been shot; he was not widely known to the public, but the Lilly drug firm was famous. Teel, thirty-seven, executive vice-president of Lilly's international division, was on the fast track to greater things. He had just been named to the board of directors of the company, which had long been a political and economic force in Indianapolis.

He had a home on Washington Boulevard worth $50,000 in 1958 dollars, had a private airplane and was a member of the elite Indianapolis Country Club, and he had not been robbed. He had $210 on him, more than chump change in that era.

Some thought him athletic, charming, handsome, rich and powerful; others considered him pompous, overbearing and always willing to use his power and money. He was married to Mary Elizabeth Roddy Teel, a Texan and an alcoholic who had met Teel in Colombia, South America, before they wed in 1932. She was a willing, but not enthusiastic, executive wife. They had one adopted son.

That's about all that was known until the next day. The presence of a 1955 Chevrolet with a white hardtop on a dirt road near Fall Creek was reported to police about 5:00 p.m., but such a thing was not a priority; it was about 8:00 p.m. before a policeman went to investigate. A woman was found curled up on her own legs in the car. With her were a vacuum bottle and two drug capsules; she had vomited and was in a coma.

Thus began the unraveling of a sordid tale of backstreet romance and betrayal. But it would be nearly two days before the details emerged, and they were so startling that they intrigued the public for days leading up to and through a riveting trial. Connie Nicholas would prompt both pity and anger as she told her story.

The identity of Connie, as she was soon called, had already been learned by the police because a swap shop owner remembered the woman; she had purchased an unusual .25-caliber French gun so complicated to use that she had required instruction. A visit to her home had uncovered a suicide note

Connie Nicholas, shown at her trial, had sympathizers and critics. Indianapolis Star *files*.

taped to the door. More suicide notes were found inside the flat, plus love letters from Teel, men's slippers and bathrobe. One note asked that the items be returned to Forrest Teel and gave his address.

Police released contents of some unsent letters they found in Connie's apartment. One, written to Teel, read:

> *I can now see that you were completely selfish in your love for me and because of this, many innocent people have been hurt.*
>
> *This has not been written in anger because I am still not angry with you, just hurt and heartbroken and my memories are of the wonderful hours that we did share and the few trips that we did take together. I am sorry that you failed me after all this time. I now know what I must do and it is something that I have given much thought to, because I have said before, life without you would have no meaning. My only fear is that I might fail—other than that I have absolutely none. Even though I know it is wrong, to me it is much easier than seeing you and knowing that I can never again be completely happy as I have been in the past.*
>
> *I still love you with all my heart and as you well know there is no halfway point for me when I truly feel as I do about you.*

Connie had also written to her second husband, Curtis Nicholas, in Detroit, saying that "by the time you get this letter I plan to no longer be in this world."

Connie recovered from her coma, though, and after some persuasion told detective Carl Michealis that she had laid in wait for Teel and shot him. An autopsy had shown that Teel had been shot in the neck, in the side and in the hip.

Meanwhile, Laura Mowrer, reading that Teel had been shot, cleaned out her desk at Lilly, where she worked as a secretary. On the advice of a lawyer, she told police her story and fled to the West Coast.

When Connie revived, she granted press interviews. What came out that Saturday, August 2, and later in the trial, was a fairly ordinary life that had gone off track for fifteen years. Connie was born in Kentucky but traveled at an early age to Oregon with her parents. Her father died when she was nine, and her struggling mother died when she was eleven. Connie lived with an uncle, W.R. Conrad, in Shelbyville, Kentucky. She worked as a housekeeper, returned to school and graduated from Shortridge High School in Indianapolis at age twenty. She worked in a cafeteria, a grocery store and a now defunct Indianapolis department store, where she became a head cashier.

I can now see that you were completely selfish in your love for me and because of this, many innocent people have been hurt.

This has not been written in anger because I am still not angry with you, just hurt and heartbroken and my memories are of the wonderful hours that we did share and the few trips that we did make together. I am sorry that you failed me after all this time.

I now know what I must do and it is something that I have given much thought to, because as I have said before, life without you would have no meaning. My only fear is that I might fail-other then that I have absolutely none. Even though I know it is wrong, to me, it is much easier then seeing you and knowing that I can never again be as completely happy as I have been in the past.

I still love you with all my heart and as you well know there is no half way point for me when I truly feel as I do about you.

*Connie*

This was one of the letters Connie Nicholas wrote that was found by police in her apartment. Indianapolis Star *files.*

In 1941, she got a job at Lilly. Connie married Ray Keifer about 1942, but they divorced. She married Curtis Nichols in the mid-1950s, but it ended in another uncontested divorce. Connie, a twenty-seven-year-old secretary at Lilly, said that she had resisted Teel's interest in her for two years but finally succumbed and started an affair. Teel paid for her apartment; she gave him a key. Marriage had been discussed, she said.

Connie accompanied Teel on trips, during which they registered as Mr. and Mrs. Teel, she said. When she learned that Teel had a new girlfriend, she began to follow him to check on it. Teel had dated other girls, she knew. They argued about it. One night, she had followed Teel to the Meadows apartments and watched him enter. A check of names on apartment mailboxes revealed one person living there who worked at Lilly, Laura Mowrer.

On the fateful night, Connie drove to the apartments, saw Teel's car, parked her own nearby and slipped into Teel's Cadillac to wait. When Teel

Connie Nicholas is questioned during her trial by an unidentified attorney. *Photo by James C. Ramsey,* Indianapolis Star *files.*

came out, he was angry; they argued, he drove Connie to her own car and they continued fighting. Teel struck her, she said, and grabbed her arm. The gun went off. Connie insisted from the start that she had gotten the gun to use on herself and that shooting Teel was an accident. She leaped out and got into her own car; Teel's Cadillac, still running, began its backward roll into the lamppost.

After that, Connie drove to the spot by the creek and ingested seventy-five sleeping pills, made by Lilly, poured into pineapple juice to make a slurry. She had prepared it for suicide. If the drugs didn't work, she planned to use the gun. But the drugs had caused her to vomit. She had been in the car, comatose, until the investigating patrolman had found her. Connie told reporters that her right hand was paralyzed because Teel had grabbed it; others claimed that the injury came because she had been lying on the arm for hours in her car.

Connie was in the hospital nearly eight months and underwent some surgeries. When she emerged, the trial was set to begin on March 16, 1959. It was held in a basement courtroom of the aging Marion County Courthouse, which was soon to be demolished. In the first week, all of the 200 jurors in the pool were dismissed. An additional 725 jurors were summoned. At last, 12 males were named jurors. All were allowed to go home at night. Testimony began on March 30 before Judge Thomas Falconer.

The courtroom, stuffy and crowded (some spectators peered in the ground-floor windows), was full of local reporters and reporters from Chicago, Louisville and New York. Wire services sent daily stories around the world.

Connie sometimes held "press conferences" at the defendant's table during a recess; there were many during legal arguments. Sometimes the jurors played bridge while waiting to return to the jury box. When Connie told her story on the witness stand, there was so much public interest that the *Indianapolis Star* printed it all verbatim, running many pages. The public was widely divided; some thought Connie was a woman wronged and Teel got what he deserved, and others thought she was a home-wrecking vixen. Judge Falconer received many letters during the trial. He said he never read any of them.

In the middle of the trial, the Marion County clerk died, halting the proceedings. Considerable political maneuvering ensued before Falconer named another clerk so the trial could proceed. Jury deliberations began at 3:30 p.m. on April 14, 1959. At 1:48 a.m., the verdict came—guilty of voluntary manslaughter.

Two days later, Connie entered the Indiana Woman's Prison, sentenced to two to twenty-one years and ordered to pay court costs of $894.65. She was released from prison during the lengthy consideration of an appeal and unsuccessful efforts to gain pauper status. She reentered prison in April 1960, almost one year after her conviction. Paroled on April 4, 1962, Connie changed her name and moved to a small town south of Indianapolis where her sister lived.

Mrs. Teel, who had moved to a new Indianapolis home, was badly burned in a fire on January 2, 1960, and died four days later. At Eli Lilly & Company, executives were sternly warned about extramarital affairs, and everyone stopped driving white Cadillacs. Some reportedly traded the "status" cars, and some had them repainted.

Thus ended the Indianapolis murder case in which the slaying was startling but the aftermath even more so, and the murderess got more attention after the homicide than the victim got alive or dead.

# Murder and Millions

Maybe if the bank hadn't embezzled Marjorie V. Jackson's money, she would not have met death at the hands of burglars in her north-side Indianapolis home that spring morning in 1977. If her slayers had not been so profligate with the millions they had stolen, they might never have been caught. Or perhaps she would have escaped being murdered if she had followed advice and helped prosecute the first burglars to break into her house. It was a case of eccentricity atop eccentricity.

Marjorie had led an unusual life before that fatal day, but when her husband Chester Jackson died in 1970, her existence went into a tailspin. With Chester she had traveled to various parts of the world, including the Holy Land, which may have been pivotal in her days of loss and grief.

Marguerite—her real name, though she always used Marjorie—was a clerk in a C.G. Murphy store in Indianapolis when she met Chester. They dated, living in the same house for perhaps twenty years before marrying in 1952. Marjorie had grown up in relative poverty. Chester was the son of L.A. Jackson, who began the city's first Standard Grocery, later sold to National Tea Company. When L.A. Jackson died, Chester inherited the chain of stores plus 25 percent of the stock in the Southwestern Coal Corporation.

Marjorie and her mother, Clara Elizabeth O'Connell, lived in Woodruff Place, a once fashionable enclave east of downtown Indianapolis. Probably about 1940, Chester and his paternal grandfather became boarders in the O'Connell home. This was shortly before Chester's first marriage ended in divorce. Woodruff Place was grand in the 1940s, and Chester brought some grandeur to the O'Connell house. Many neighbors thought that Chester and Marjorie were man and wife; they got a marriage license in 1952. Marjorie, too, had been married previously. Soon, Chester and Marjorie moved to Spring Mill Road, a newer upscale neighborhood in northwest Indianapolis.

There, more splendors were installed. There were several cars. The home had three grand pianos. Although frivolous in number, Marjorie used the pianos. Chester had taken her many places to study with renowned piano instructors. Marjorie also began to meditate extensively.

Oddities started early. Chester often worked late, and neighbors remembered Marjorie turning on all the lights at Woodruff Place and letting out the guard dogs. But little was thought of it. Chester had his troubles. Once he spent time in an Indianapolis sanitarium for what some termed a nervous breakdown. When he died, the scene was set for disaster.

Chester's estate was an estimated $14 million. Two years later, the estate acquired one-fourth of the $58,220,000 realized from the sale of the coal company's stock. Marjorie's inheritance was placed in the hands of Herbert Biddle Jr., a trust officer with Indiana National Bank. Soon Marjorie began to think that she was being swindled—how is unclear, but it may have involved the manner in which interest was paid on her investment.

This is a snapshot of Marjorie Jackson taken years before the widowed heiress was robbed and killed. Indianapolis Star *files*.

The sixty-six-year-old woman began to remove money from the bank. In February 1976, bank officials sought a guardianship to protect her funds. However, the guardianship was denied when it was found that Biddle had indeed taken $700,000 from Marjorie's trust fund, skimming from the $9 million left in her account after taxes, attorney fees and other expenses at Chester's death. Her faith crushed, Marjorie started escalating withdrawals and taking the money home.

Marjorie had a precedent. Chester was known to have kept large amounts of cash at the house. Soon, $500,000 withdrawals rose to $1 million, and one day Marjorie withdrew $2 million, closing the account. She carried it home in a bag in her white Cadillac. Such hoarding could not go long without notice.

# Catalogue of Slaughter

On May 7, 1977, firemen were called to investigate a fire at the Jackson property. They found Marjorie dead, shot in the abdomen with a .22-caliber pistol. Later, a series of events showed the trail to murder.

One day in May 1976, a man broke into Marjorie's attached garage, worked through the ceiling crawl space into the house and opened the door for a waiting partner. The pair took a suitcase from a hall closet. Police later learned that the suitcase contained $817,000. They also learned that a flower shop clerk who knew Marjorie had abetted the burglars. The criminals spent too much, too fast, and too many "friends" learned about the crime. Soon, a grand jury indicted the culprits.

Officials went to Marjorie with the case. They were rebuked. Marjorie had become a recluse. She had let the grass grow to weeds and had built a fence. She required deliverymen to honk and give her packages over the fence. Marjorie told authorities that the burglary must have been "God's will." The burglars went unpunished without her testimony.

But among those who heard about the burglary was Howard R. Willard of Mooresville, thirty-eight, an unemployed former hospital maintenance worker who had served time for grand larceny, second-degree burglary and theft. He recruited Manuel L. Robinson, twenty-eight, a black man from inner city Indianapolis recently released after serving seven years for burglary. Willard contacted the flower shop worker who had steered the earlier burglars.

On May 1, 1977, Robinson and Willard entered the Jackson home in the first of five burglaries. Marjorie was out. The next day, Robinson and a friend named John A. Williams paid $7,000 cash for a Pontiac Trans Am. The burglaries continued, always when Marjorie was away. But on the night of the fifth burglary, Marjorie surprised the intruders and was shot to death. One or both of the burglars returned to the Jackson home early on Saturday, May 7, 1977, and set it afire, hoping to conceal their crime.

Arriving firemen discovered Marjorie's body on the kitchen floor, wearing pajama bottoms and a flannel robe. Police discovered the gunshot wounds, and they also found what eventually totaled $5 million in garbage cans, drawers, closets, toolboxes and a vacuum cleaner bag. The cash was in consecutively numbered $100 bills, and there also were $1 silver certificates considered collector's items. The murderers had overlooked more than they took. Still, it was considered one of the largest burglary heists in the world, and the story circled the globe.

Investigators also found furs hanging in the garage, a freezer full of cheese, a table set for a banquet, cakes and gift-wrapped packages containing small items such as washcloths and bearing tags reading "To Jesus Christ from Marjorie Jackson" and "To God from Marjorie." Acquaintances said of Marjorie near the end that she was spending six days a week in worship. She had spent nights in her bedroom meditating and talking with God, they said.

Homicide detectives learned Robinson was flashing money. Willard had done nearly the same thing, buying drinks in his favorite Mooresville tavern. He also had purchased two cars and wrecked both.

When Robinson returned to an Indianapolis car dealer to complain about a scratch on the new car he had bought with $10,000 cash, police were waiting. They tailed him and arrested Robinson and a girlfriend riding with him in his new car. Willard and his ex-wife, Marjorie Pollitt, had gone west, towing a twenty-six-foot trailer behind their 1972 car. They were seized in Phoenix on May 20, where they had purchased a $35,000 motor home. They had $170,000 on them.

Marjorie's money was found all over the place, included buried in the desert and with friends and relatives of the killers. It was thought that Robinson had $300,000 buried somewhere and never recovered it, although he asked for a pauper attorney at his trial.

Willard was sentenced to life, plus fifteen years for murder, burglary and arson. Robinson, oddly, was found not guilty of the murder but guilty of burglary and arson. He was released from prison in May 1988. Mrs. Pollitt was sentenced to five years for conspiracy to transport stolen money interstate. Her sister, Robertina Harroll Anderson, in whose Georgia home nearly $4,000 of the loot was found, got two and a half years on the same charge.

In a melancholy postscript, items from Chester's bedroom were offered for sale in May 1978. Workmen had acquired them when Marjorie, who had never entered the bedroom after Chester's death, ordered five truckloads of property hauled away. It included 150 pair of shoes. The workmen were given the material in addition to money for cleaning out the bedroom. In December that year, items from Marjorie Jackson's estate were offered in a booth at an antique and collectible show and sale in Anderson. They had been purchased at auction.

By then, of course, it made no difference to Marjorie. To those who believe in such things, she was by then with the Lord she had so fervently worshiped before being sent to him by a bullet.

# Matrimonial Murder

Occasionally a convicted killer, wishing to set the record straight or relieve guilt, reveals undiscovered homicides. Such was the case of Edmund J. Cody. Serving a life term for one murder, he revealed six other murders for which he was responsible—four of them for which he never had been charged and three of them involving his former wives. "I'm getting older. I'd like to clear my conscience and, really, I found religion," he told a newspaper reporter visiting him at the Indiana State Prison in 1980.

Cody had been married to eight women, twice to one of them. He said he killed two of his exes and helped get rid of a third ex-wife after she had been slain by a friend. He had forgotten the name of one of his victims. The crime for which he was serving time was so obvious that there were few extenuating circumstances. It, too, involved a woman: Cody's girlfriend.

On March 15, 1970, Cody walked into a White Castle restaurant in Indianapolis, dragged Flossie Crawley outside and began beating her. Cody thought he had a relationship with Crawley. So did William Love, who was inside the restaurant. When Love saw Cody draw a handgun and shoot Crawley in the chest, Love ran to her aid. Love, suddenly fearing for his own life, tried to flee back into the restaurant, but Cody shot him fatally. Cody fled in a friend's 1959 Chevrolet.

Cody was arrested later at a wrecker company at which he was employed, and the car was removed by police and taken to a wrecking storage lot. Not until May 18 did employees at the wrecking company find the decomposed body of a woman in the trunk of Cody's getaway car. It was the body of Letha Gay Morrison Cody, who had been reported missing. Cody, awaiting trial, denied killing Letha but later admitted it.

Letha had been Cody's sixth wife. Cody was a muscular man of fifty-eight years at the time of his confessions, with sandy hair flecked with gray and standing five feet, nine inches tall. He was a graduate of Ben Davis High School in Indianapolis and had a pockmarked face, big ears, a sly grin and a theory that his charm attracted women to him. His string of marital violence seemed to begin in November 1950. But before that, he admitted killing a soldier in 1944 in a Cincinnati bar fight. Cody had forgotten, if he ever knew, the name of the victim. He said he had "cut" the soldier earlier, and when the soldier left the hospital, he went looking for Cody. "I killed him in a knife fight," Cody said.

Cody had wed Ella Mae Voiles in 1941, divorcing her in 1945. In 1946, he was married to Ruth Dunham. Cody told the reporter he and Ruth never divorced, but he believed that she had moved to another city and married. In 1949, Cody married Ella Mae again. She was found frozen to death on a farm where she lived near New Castle. Evidently, Ella Mae and Ruth escaped being killed by Cody.

In 1950, Cody met Helen Mallette. He shot her to death in a car on the west side of Indianapolis. Then Cody shot himself in the chest, perhaps in remorse. For Mallette's slaying, Cody was tried in Morgan County, but the jury could not agree on murder and convicted him of manslaughter. Cody was sentenced to two to twenty-one years in prison; he served three years.

Before that murder, Cody had a string of arrests dating back to 1938, including passing bad checks, theft and assault and battery. In 1945, he was sentenced to four years in federal prison in Terre Haute for interstate transportation of stolen cars. Not long after his release for the Mallette slaying, Cody again was convicted of interstate transportation of stolen cars. He served 582 days.

In February 1958, Cody married Dorothy Lee Shaffer Cody. She was shot to death three months later by her former husband. The next wife was Geraldine Bishop Wilkins, whom Cody married in 1960. Cody said he killed her with a hammer in an argument and dumped her body in Jefferson County, Kentucky. He wrapped the body in a blanket and put it in the back of a station wagon, loading in the vehicle her three children by a former marriage and telling them they were going to relatives in Georgia. While traveling on I-65 south of Louisville, Cody said a wreck halted him.

"So I took Geraldine out of the car when the traffic was stopped for the accident and threw her down the ravine. The kids didn't know what I threw away," Cody said. He then took the children to the home of Geraldine's brother in Cedar Bluff, Alabama.

Geraldine's body, dressed in blue panties, was found in the summer of 1965 but was not identified until Cody's confession. Cody was indicted for the murder of Geraldine, but the charges were dismissed because of lack of evidence and a request for a speedy trial.

Evelyn Parsley married Cody in 1966 and was reported missing three years later. The woman, an employee in a baby ward at Methodist Hospital, was murdered by a friend, Cody said. The woman encountered Cody and the friend engaged in a homosexual act in the apartment Cody and Evelyn shared in southern Marion County. Cody said he tried to dissuade Evelyn from calling the police, urging her to forget about what she had seen. The friend, whom Cody declined to identify, pulled out a .22-caliber revolver and shot Evelyn to death. "I helped carry her body to the trunk of the car," said

Cody. He claimed that they drove to a field near Covington, Kentucky. The body never has been found.

That same year, 1969, Cody married Letha Gay. He provided few details about Letha Gay's murder but admitted that he had strangled her in March 1970 during a struggle in their home. This happened before the White Castle slaying that put him in prison for life. Cody said he put Letha Gay's body in the trunk of the 1959 Chevrolet but neglected to dispose of it. That was the body the wrecker storage employees found.

Cody also recalled being married for a short time to Mary Ann Rader Cody and Ruth Kruse Cody in the late 1950s or early 1960s. Their whereabouts were unknown, but Cody told the reporter that, as far as he knew in 1980, Mary Ann and Ruth were still alive somewhere.

At any rate, they were among the three former Cody wives he didn't kill. In 1980, behind prison walls, Cody confided that his visitors included a woman from northern Indiana, whose name he declined to divulge. Nor did he say whether his new "friend" knew how Cody's eight marriages had turned out nor whether she, too, was attracted by his charm.

# Just Like Something in the Movies

Alfred Henry Smith, seventy-one years old, did what most normal people do when gunfire erupts: he rose to flee. That's when Smith, who was having an early lunch with his wife, became a happenstance murder victim. His wife, Linda, held him in her arms for an hour after she heard his last gasp of life. Although not slain or wounded, she was also part of one of the most bizarre hostage homicides in Indianapolis history.

It began about 11:00 a.m. on Monday, May 23, 1994, at a Denny's restaurant on Pendleton Pike in northeast Indianapolis and didn't end until nearly 5:00 p.m. that day; four people were wounded and a parade of hostages was freed during the incident. Finally surrendering were two brothers fleeing from a theft charge in Casper, Wyoming, who had picked Indianapolis almost at random as a bus ride destination in their flight.

Alfred Smith and his wife had chosen the restaurant at random. They did not dine there regularly. Undoubtedly, others among the numerous patrons were also there by chance, although some may have been "regulars." Whether the gunmen planned a robbery is uncertain. They did have only about one dollar between them, had ordered food for which they could not pay and were armed with a .357 Magnum and 9mm semiautomatic assault pistol.

Thomas E. Mathisen, twenty-four, and his brother Ronald Jr., twenty-seven, had purchased weapons from a private dealer before leaving Casper. They had been in an Indianapolis motel for three days and chose the Denny's, they said, because it was nearby.

Robert Doan, forty-nine, a Denny's manager, was also in the restaurant by happenstance. He had come there to interview a prospective employee. His encounter with the edgy Mathisen brothers was accidental, too. Tom Mathisen was moving to the back of the restaurant when he bumped into Doan. Tom's gun went off twice, perhaps accidentally, the bullets hitting Doan in the stomach and buttock. When that occurred, Ronald panicked and began shooting wildly at least six times with his revolver. One slug went through Alfred Smith's arm and into his chest, killing him. Four other restaurant patrons were wounded. Bedlam broke loose. "It was just like something you see in the movies," said one of the restaurant cooks, "but it wasn't a movie."

Alfred Smith, a World War I army veteran, had been a retired car salesman and former self-employed carpenter. Later during the standoff, when the gunmen were in telephone contact with police, they said that they were sending out Smith's dead body because they "couldn't stand it." Two hostages were allowed to open the restaurant door and place Smith's body outside on the grass.

The wounded, besides Doan, were Justin Basicker, five; Steve Johnson, twenty-three; and Cecil Williams, seventy-five. During the standoff, the Mathisen brothers expressed remorse for the situation. They later admitted that they had planned to rob people in Indianapolis, commit murders to eliminate witnesses and then perhaps take their own lives. Suicide seemed to be personal atonement for their problems.

In Casper, Tom Mathisen had been manager of an adult video store and bookstore, and his brother had been an employee. When the pair stole about $4,000 they were supposed to deposit, they decided to flee. It wasn't their first illegal act. In 1999, they had stolen from a pizza restaurant at which Ron had worked. They fled to Redding, California, and then surrendered on a theft charge. They were given probation. Tom had also served six months in Wyoming and a year's probation for stealing cars.

Now, thieves again, they bought the two guns and drove to Cheyenne, Wyoming; Lincoln, Nebraska; Council Bluff, Iowa; and Des Moines, Iowa, where they abandoned their car. They took out a map, spotted Indianapolis and decided to go there by bus. Details were lacking on how they reached the Denny's area, several miles from the downtown Indianapolis bus depot, or how they chose it.

When the Denny's shooting began, several employees and customers were able to flee. As time wore on and police negotiators made contact, the gunmen released hostages a few at a time. Police learned about Tom Mathisen's pregnant wife, Heather, in Casper and told him they had talked to her. Tom telephoned her at least twice from inside the restaurant. Conversations with her played a part in the brothers' surrender, police said.

By the time the pair surrendered, only about seven of the approximate twenty-five hostages originally in the restaurant were still being held. At one point, male customers were allowed to evacuate some wounded but were forced to return; the brothers had threatened to shoot their wives if they didn't comply.

At 5:07 p.m., the two gunmen and the remaining hostages walked out of the restaurant. Thus one of the city's most startling hostage standoffs ended somewhat peacefully. But it left behind four persons with gunshot wounds and Alfred Smith as victim of a wildly unplanned homicide.

Eventually, Tom and Ron Mathisen pleaded guilty to murder, attempted murder, attempted robbery and confinement. Each was sentenced to life without parole plus three hundred years.

# Death of a Fighter

It is unlikely that the gunman who attacked Joseph E. Horvath late that Friday night on May 11, 1956, knew the background of the man he was about to kill. Horvath, thirty-three years old, was not a man who gave up easily. Never mind that his wife, Marcia, thirty, and his children—Andrew, six, and Susan, four—were present, giving him enough motive to resist and therefore possibly save them from death or injury. In addition, before Horvath came to live on the west side of Indianapolis, he had been a Hungarian freedom fighter. A man who in 1956 had battled Russian tanks in his homeland probably would be stalwart against a gunman who leaped into his car.

In fact, Horvath did meet his unexpected death fighting. It was shortly before midnight when Horvath, driving the family station wagon, neared his home on Ketcham Street in Indianapolis. He and his wife and children had been to a drive-in movie, as police later learned, and the children were asleep in the back of the car. As the Horvaths neared the yard of friend and sometime fishing companion David Wingler, Mrs. Horvath rolled down the passenger window and bent forward in the front seat to pick up shoes on the car floor.

When she looked up, she saw a man poking what was believed to have been a .45-caliber pistol in the window. "I'm going to kill you," he told Horvath as he slid into the vehicle. "Keep driving." The intruder said to keep the children in the back. When Horvath asked what was going on, the man said, "I'm not kidding. This ain't no game."

Horvath, his wife said, twice offered the gunman money, the car or "everything I've got." The gunman kept insisting that it was no game and that he was going to kill Horvath.

When six-year-old David was awakened, he blurted out that his father had a gun, although that was untrue. At that moment, Horvath reached across his wife, grabbed the assailant's arm and began to grapple with him. The gun went off, shooting a hole in the car's roof. "You're not going to kill me or any of my family," Horvath shouted. Then the car door came open, and both men fell to the ground. As they wrestled, Mrs. Horvath told police, the assailant fired once at close range. The bullet entered Horvath's chest on the left side.

The struggle had taken the two men onto the lawn of the Wingler house, only a few doors from the Horvath residence. Wingler told police later that he had heard the first shot but thought it was a firecracker. When the second shot sounded, he and his wife rushed outside. That's when Mrs. Horvath cried to Wingler's wife, "Sandra, he's shot Joe." By the time Wingler reached Horvath, he was dead and the gunman had fled.

Horvath—who had survived the fighting in Hungary, had escaped from Eastern Europe and made his home in Indianapolis—had been killed by a man Mrs. Horvath described as wild and screaming. Police theorized that the assailant was possibly under the influence of narcotics and probably bent on robbery.

On the Sunday after the slaying, Mrs. Horvath examined crime file photographs at police headquarters. She had described the slayer as a slender black man, twenty to thirty years old and about six feet tall. Investigators were linking the murder to other crimes in the area. A man had been robbed at gunpoint in the Horvaths' neighborhood only an hour earlier. Another victim had reported that a black man armed with a .38-caliber revolver had accosted him in his car only a few blocks from the Horvath home and had taken the car, money and a watch. Some three months earlier, a victim had been shot and wounded when a gunman waited in a garage and tried to rob the garage owner when he came home.

Mrs. Horvath, however, was unable to help police assemble a composite photo of the man who killed her husband. Not only did she have a heart ailment and was distraught, but she also had been struck on the head with the killer's weapon.

Police also were delayed in their investigation because an autopsy was not performed quickly on Horvath; the body reached examiners on Sunday. But they did find fingerprints of the killer in the car. A tipster provided information that led to an arrest.

Several men were seized in May 1969, one year after the Horvath murder. They were linked to that case and several other crimes. Among them was Richard A. Emerson. Mrs. Horvath immediately identified him as her husband's assailant and repeated that identification at Emerson's trial in April 1970.

He was convicted and sentenced to life in prison.

# They Didn't Send Flowers

If it hadn't been for the neighbors, there might have been two murders that June night in 1944. Only Gus L. Weidenhoft, sixty-five years old, was beaten to death before police, notified by neighbors, arrived at his home on South Meridian Street in Indianapolis. His wife Carrie, fifty-nine, was also savagely beaten, but she survived to tell investigators what happened when two men, bent on robbery, entered their home about 11:00 p.m. on that Friday night, June 30.

The Weidenhofts were well-known florists in the area. Carrie had operated a flower stand at City Market for quite a while. It also was known by their friends and neighbors that they kept considerable money in their home to make change for flower sales. Carrie had been talking that night on the front porches of some of her neighbors across the street. Gus was seated on his own front porch waiting for his wife to return home.

She did at about 10:30 p.m., after chatting with Mr. and Mrs. A. DeLoss Acheson and Mr. and Mrs. Frank Schneider. Acheson told police that when he retired soon thereafter he saw, from his upstairs bedroom, the lights come on in the Weidenhoft house. When he saw strange men in the Weidenhoft home, he called police. They arrived, later investigation showed, while the murderers-robbers still were looking for more cash. Evidently hearing the patrol car, they fled.

Police found Carrie, in her pajamas and housecoat, collapsed on a davenport in the living room, beaten insensible. She had been struck at least three times, and an attempt had been made to strangle her with curtains.

Upstairs, police found Gus dead on the hallway floor. He had been struck ten times or more with a blunt object, later revealed to have been a lug wrench, the same weapon that had been used against his wife. Gus had also been struck with a handgun. A coroner's investigation showed that the fatal blow to Weidenhoft was above the right ear, which caused an eight-inch fracture. He also suffered a crushed jaw, skull and chin. Three bullets, which probably fell from the handgun, were found on the floor. The splintered panel in the bedroom door and evidence inside the room showed that the two-hundred-pound Gus had fought his killers.

Carrie rallied from her injuries and by July 3 was able to tell investigators the events of that night. She said that she was upstairs when her husband answered the door and admitted a man who asked to see Mrs. Weidenhoft. The caller said that he and his companion had ordered flowers earlier in the day. Carrie came downstairs, passing her pajama-clad husband as he went upstairs. One of the two men, both strangers to her, made a motion to shake hands. When she complied, she said,

The home in which Gus Wiedenhoft was killed and his wife beaten still stands on the south side of Indianapolis. *Photo by author.*

she was struck with the lug wrench once, and then the assailant tried to strangle her with drapes from a nearby window. That failing, he struck her twice more, and she fell in a daze.

The last thing she recalled was her husband saying, "You can't do that." Mrs. Weidenhoft told police that the two men looked Italian—one had a mustache, they both wore brown suits and both were hatless. Mrs. Weidenhoft offered a $1,000 reward for finding the killers of her husband.

Evidence showed that the gunmen had taken Weidenhoft's wallet containing about $200. However, the intruders missed more than $1,200 hidden around the house, including change in cans on the living room table. Footprints outside indicated that the slayers had jumped from the kitchen window.

Neighbors reported having seen a car parked on Tabor Street behind the Weidenhoft home and had heard one, seemingly in need of a tune-up, speed away. One report was that the car contained three men.

Neighbors were shocked, not only because of the savagery of the slaying, but also because the Weidenhofts were well known and liked. Gus had money around the house not only for transactions in the adjacent greenhouse, but also because he habitually paid his bills in cash. "Cold Cash Gus" was a nickname some had applied to him.

Weidenhoft had been born in Chicago, where he had learned the flower business. He had worked at that trade in several towns before the couple came to Indianapolis in 1928, moving into their home on South Meridian Street, at the time a very upscale brick residence. The couple had been married for forty-one years. Mrs. Weidenhoft was known to thousands who patronized her flower stand at City Market, a busy downtown marketplace.

The day after the slaying, the bloodied lug wrench and a .32-caliber Smith and Wesson were found near the greenhouse, believed discarded by the fleeing killers. Loose talk in a tavern ninety-three days later led to the arrest of thirty-three-year-old Charles DeGraffenreed, who was positively identified by Mrs. Weidenhoft as the smaller of her two assailants. Within hours a second suspect, Ryan Woodson, was also seized. The two were once hired by Gus Weidenhoft to clean the walls and shades in the Weidenhoft home, police learned. Authorities also learned that the gun found near the greenhouse had been stolen from a woman on north Capitol Avenue about four months before Gus was killed. DeGraffenreed had been heard talking about "killing a man" while in a tavern on Indiana Avenue, police said, and had an injured ankle.

When DeGraffenreed went to trial on March 7, 1945, the prosecution asked for the death penalty. Two witnesses said that DeGraffenreed was asked in a restaurant why he was limping, and in response, he showed them a newspaper story of the Weidenhoft slaying.

DeGraffenreed's alibi witnesses said that he had been at a tavern and, later, at a party at a private home on West Twenty-eighth Street, a long way from the Weidenhoft home the night of the slaying. But the prosecution offered witnesses who disputed that claim.

On March 14, DeGraffenreed was found guilty of murder by a jury that deliberated seven hours. When the jury was told to fix a penalty, a two-hour debate resulted in seven calling for the death penalty. But in the end the panel of eleven women and one man settled on a sentence of life; the judge complied.

## Jesus, Take These Children

As tragic as murders can be, sometimes the aftermath seems equally dire. The killings committed by King Edward Bell fit into that category. Not only did Bell kill all four of his own children, their mother and their grandmother, he also later took his own life in prison.

On Sunday, August 16, 1981, Bell took his four children to Mass at an Indianapolis church. He had custody of the youngsters. On the next Friday, he killed them all; he had told friends that he would rather see them dead than mistreated. The victims, according to their birth certificates, were King Edwin Bell II, five years old; Bertina LaShell Bell, four; Berkina Mishell Bell, three; and Kingston Edmond Bell III, one. The slayer said that he disapproved of his estranged wife's treatment of the children and her relationship with her new boyfriend.

After shooting the children, Bell, thirty-one years old and a Vietnam War veteran, tracked down his wife, Bertha Mae Bell, at the home of her mother, Mary Alice Kirby, fifty-four, and killed both of them. He also tried to kill Bertha Mae's boyfriend, Clarence Barnett. At the time it was the largest mass murder in Indianapolis history, although it later was surpassed.

Bell's twenty-six-year-old wife had filed for divorce. He was financially strapped. He had been laid off for two years from his job at a foundry, although he recently had found another job. Colleagues at the foundry where Bell once worked said that he was quiet and, when not working, read the Bible. None of his acquaintances thought him capable of killing. Their diagnosis was that he just snapped.

Police discovered the gruesome slaying of the children because of Bell's killing of his estranged wife and mother-in-law. When he found that his wife had not arrived for work at a restaurant, police learned, he had gone looking for her and eventually turned to Barnett. As the fifty-one-year-old Barnett drove out of a parking lot near his apartment, Bell fired three shotgun blasts through the windshield of Barnett's car. Barnett was critically wounded. That incident brought police to that scene.

Bell then drove to a parking lot near the Crossroads Rehabilitation Center in Indianapolis where, police said, he found his wife. Bell shot her several times, using both a shotgun and a handgun, and then went into the nearby home of his mother-in-law. Coming out of the house, leaving Mrs. Kirby dead on the floor between the living and dining rooms, Bell shot his wife once more, according to witnesses. Two adults and a child in Mrs. Kirby's

A photo, found in the home, revealed the children killed by King Edward Bell. Indianapolis Star *files*.

house were unharmed. Bell was on his mother-in-law's front porch with the shotgun when police arrived there about 7:30 a.m. on Friday, August 21.

Once they learned the address of Bell's residence, police went there, broke in a side door and found the dead children. They were dressed in nightclothes, covered with blankets and lying on bunk beds in the basement. Three of the children had been shot once in the head; the youngest was shot four times, including once in the hand, perhaps trying to ward off his father. It was believed that the children had been killed about 2:00 a.m. On the wall near their bodies, Bell had written in chalk: "Jesus, take these children." Other religious comments in chalk, plus obscene references to Bell's wife, were found around the house. A photo album of the family was found open on the sofa.

Bell and his wife had been married for eight years. In 1959, he had come to Indianapolis from New Albany, where he had attended school. He was one of fourteen children. In June 1969, he had joined the army and served two tours in Vietnam.

Bell was jailed under constant surveillance. On the Saturday after the slayings, he asked the court to be put to death. But prosecutors pointed out that mass murder in itself does not justify the death penalty. In the period leading up to the trial, Bell, who pleaded guilty to the murders but mentally ill, tried several times to commit suicide, once with an overdose of aspirin. While in jail he also wrote a diary called "Story of God and Devil (Demon or Angel) Mass Murder or Insane Sickness?" In the diary, Bell portrayed himself as a mistreated husband and a devout servant of God. He blamed his wife, his in-laws and society for the nightmare created by his earthly demons. Experts were divided on whether Bell could be treated successfully for his problems.

In the end, he was sentenced in 1982 to forty years for each of the children and forty years for the murders of his wife and mother-in-law. The sentences were to run concurrently. Bell was sent to the Indiana State Prison at Michigan City.

Shortly before 7:00 p.m. on Sunday, July 5, 1987, Bell was found dead when a prison worker delivered the evening meal to his cell. Over his head he put a plastic bag that he had concealed under a blanket. Bell left no suicide note. He was thirty-seven years old. Commented Bell's attorney on hearing of the suicide, "Maybe he has found peace."

# Concrete Evidence

In a murder case that stretched from Noblesville, through Indianapolis and finally to Missouri, the killings did not become evident until the suspected slayers were halted on the highway. The traffic stop spurred Missouri police to urge Indianapolis authorities to investigate a house on Linwood Avenue on the east side of Indianapolis. There, shortly before noon on February 8, 2005, recently poured concrete was found in the basement of the home where ninety-one-year-old Leander Bradley lived with his seventy-five-year-old wife, Betty.

Use of $10,000 electronic equipment showed the presence of an unknown mass under the fresh concrete. A cadaver-sniffing dog indicated the presence of human remains. Excavation revealed thirteen black plastic bags containing parts of murdered people. Investigators believed that the Bradleys were among the body parts, along with Sharon Allen, their daughter.

About 11:00 a.m. on February 8, a car was pulled over on Interstate 70 in Missouri for speeding and other violations. The car had been stopped near St. Louis by a drug and crime interdiction unit watching for suspicious vehicles. In the car were Kenneth Lee Allen, twenty-nine, and his sister, Kari A. Allen, eighteen. They were Sharon Allen's children. Kenneth, who was driving, appeared nervous, Missouri deputies said.

Officers said questions brought differing responses from Kenneth and his sister. When asked about drugs, investigators said, Kenneth gave permission to search the rented 2005 Chevrolet. The search turned up credit card statements, a satchel filled with jewelry, bloody pillows, a sheet in a trash bag and driver's licenses of the Bradleys.

While investigators were alerting Indianapolis police to check on the Bradleys, Kari told Missouri police that her mother and grandparents had been killed. Some police checked the Bradley home, while others went to the Noblesville apartment of Sharon Allen. Questioning and further investigation revealed this scenario.

In November 2004, Allen—who had served time in Kentucky for counterfeiting and was on probation for fraud and theft charges in Florida—and his sister began trying to enlist their mother Sharon in a scheme: to raid the home of Allen's grandparents to get $200,000 that the Bradleys had saved. The money evidently was wanted for a gambling spree in Las Vegas. When Mrs. Allen refused to take part, she was stabbed to death in her apartment about December 30. The body was dismembered and placed in a plastic bag.

Then, according to police, Mrs. Bradley was lured to Sharon Allen's apartment by being told that Mrs. Allen was ill. When she arrived, she was suffocated, dismembered and also placed in a plastic bag. Kenneth and Kari went to the Bradley home and waited for Leander's arrival. When he came home, he was killed by hammer blows to the head.

During the first week of January, according to neighbors, an electric jackhammer and bags of cement were seen being carried into the Bradley house. For several days, a van was seen at the house and noises, lasting all night, suggested construction in the Bradley home. One neighbor said it sounded as if sewer repair was underway.

It was at this time, according to investigators, that the bodies of Sharon Allen and Betty Bradley were carried from Noblesville to the Bradley house and placed in a basement hole, along with the body of Leander Bradley. Then the hole was filled with concrete.

The next event in the bizarre case was the traffic stop in Missouri.

Kenneth Allen, facing charges of murder and the death penalty, sought to have the evidence gained in search of his grandparents' home suppressed on the basis that the police lacked a proper search warrant. Prosecutors countered that police went to the Bradley home because the call from Missouri caused them to think the couple might be in danger. The judge in the case denied the requested suppression of the discovery of the bodies. Allen pleaded guilty in January 2010 to three counts of murder to avoid the death penalty. He was sentenced on February 5 to life without parole plus 130 years. Kari Allen, who admitted being the lookout in the crimes, pleaded guilty to three counts of conspiracy. She was sentenced to 38 years in prison, plus 2 years in community corrections programs, on April 9, 2010.

# The Indianapolis Massacre

About 10:15 p.m. on Thursday, June 1, 2006, neighbors in the 500 block of North Hamilton Avenue in Indianapolis heard screaming from a nearby house and gunshots, perhaps ten or twelve of them. Arriving police found that four adults and three children had been slain. It was the worst homicide in Indianapolis history.

Dead were Alberto Covarrubias, fifty-six, and two of his children—David, eleven, and Alberto, eight. Also dead were Emma Valdez (who lived with Covarrubias), her daughter Flora Albarran, twenty-two; her son Magno

Albarran, twenty-nine; and Flora's son Luis Albarran, five. The three children had been killed in one bed in a back bedroom. They were face-down. Covarrubias and Emma Valdez were face-down on the dining room floor. Magno and Flora died in the kitchen. Each victim had been shot in the head and also in the body.

Police found thirty shell casings in the house, all 7.62mm, ammunition typically used in military weapons. Emma Valdez, who worked at a day-care center and a cemetery, had arrived from Mexico fifteen years earlier. Emma met Alberto, and they brought their children together and had two of their own, David and Alberto.

Besides his maintenance job, Covarrubias bought homes, fixed them up and rented them. Covarrubias had his own home other than the Hamilton Avenue address and didn't always stay there. But he had decided to stay on that fateful night.

Magno Albarran, a bricklayer, lived with his mother Emma but, on the night of the slaying, planned to take his girlfriend to the movies. He had taken his daughter, Jasmine, to the child's mother before going back home to change his clothes.

Flora, who did not live at the Hamilton Avenue address, had left her son, Luis, there while she ran errands. She had returned about 10:00 p.m. to pick up the child.

The slain children were on their first day of summer vacation from school. Alberto had just finished fifth grade. David had just finished with second grade. Luis had just been registered to attend kindergarten in the fall.

Investigators soon discovered that the murders resulted from a robbery gone wrong. According to neighborhood rumor, there was lots of money (some rumors said $47,000) and cocaine hidden in the Hamilton Avenue house. It wasn't true.

The next day, police stopped James Stewart, thirty, at a traffic light. They had received a tip that he might have been involved. His seizure provided a clear picture of the murder, police said.

With Stewart in custody, police began interviewing friends and relatives of Desmond Turner. More than one hundred policemen were searching, joined by the FBI and other federal agencies. Their search led to a female acquaintance of Turner's who said that he had borrowed her GMC pickup and told her he "needed to make some money." In her house, police found clothing similar to those Turner reportedly wore the night of the killings.

Turner, twenty-eight, had a long criminal record and had been released in the fall of 2005 after serving three and a half years in prison on drug and weapon charges. Hearing that he was wanted, Turner turned himself in to a policeman he knew at a fast-food restaurant near downtown Indianapolis shortly before 7:00 p.m. on Saturday, less than forty-eight hours after the massacre.

Believing that there was cash and cocaine in the house, investigators said, Turner planned to borrow a truck, find an accomplice (which he did in Stewart) and kill everybody in the house. Turner had also heard that there was a safe in the murder house.

According to police, Turner and Stewart knocked at the Hamilton Avenue house and were admitted. About the same time, Magno arrived with takeout food, and Flora Albarran entered through the front door to pick up her five-year-old son. That's when the shooting began.

Turner and Stewart were both charged with murder in the case, plus two dozen other charges. The death penalty was at first sought against Turner but not Stewart.

The death penalty against Turner was withdrawn, in part because there was no physical evidence obtained at the murder scene. As a result of plea bargaining, Turner opted out of a jury trial and was tried before the judge. During the trial of Stewart, jurors visited the Hamilton County neighborhood but did not enter the burned-out murder house. Oddly, the home had been set afire in what investigators said was arson on August 23, 2008.

Based primarily on circumstantial evidence, Turner was found guilty and was sentenced on November 20, 2009, to life plus 88 years; he vowed to appeal. Stewart was found guilty on December 11 and was sentenced to a total of 425 years on January 6, 2010. He also vowed to appeal.

# From the Stage to the Grave

If relatives in California hadn't become concerned about trying to reach Leanne Paulsen in her Carmel home, there is no telling when her body would have been found. But police, sent to the home as a result of unsuccessful telephone calls, discovered Leanne's body on April 18, 2007, concealed in a crawl space, its door blocked by inline skates and storage bins. She was naked, face-down on the floor and had been killed by blows to the head.

The body was somewhat mummified, and investigators believed that she had been dead a week or longer. In the house, her sixteen-month-old son Christopher was found crying in his crib. Four hours later, police found Leanne's husband, John James Paulsen, wandering in the street some distance from the house. He told police that he was looking for his wife, saying that she had been out drinking and wandered away. J.J., as Paulsen was known, was seized on a charge of neglect of a dependent involving the child in the crib.

Thus began a story of murder that was more startling because of those involved, a vivacious former homecoming queen who had toured the nation in the cast of well-known musicals and a husband who had a distinguished career as a television writer.

The couple had twice been involved in domestic abuse situations, and Leanne had become reclusive after her pregnancy. There had been financial difficulties, leading to foreclosure proceedings on the home by lenders seeking $700,000. There had been some alcohol problems, and J.J. was on probation for domestic assault. The murder, though, was a scenario more dramatic than anything Paulsen had written for television.

Police soon charged Paulsen, forty-seven, with the murder of his thirty-nine-year-old wife of less than three and a half years. An autopsy revealed that Leanne had died of bleeding in the brain caused by the blows; she had been struck many times, and some injuries had been inflicted after Leanne was dead, investigators determined.

Police said that there was evidence of a struggle in the Paulsen home near 106th Street north of the Marion County line. A splintered and broken bed frame was found in the upstairs master bedroom, and there were dents and fractures in the wallboard there.

Investigation in the case quickly focused on the background of J.J. and Leanne. She had been stopped in November 2006 while driving her 2002 black Mercedes-Benz. When her blood-alcohol test showed 0.23, she was charged with operating a motor vehicle while intoxicated. The case was pending when her body was found. J.J. was being sued for nonpayment of the lease on his $80,000 Jaguar and also for the home mortgage and fees at the Woodland Country Club, among other debts. Almost $620,000 was being sought on the mortgage on the home into which they had moved early in 2004. In October 2006, J.J. had been arrested for slapping Leanne; he pleaded guilty in January 2007 and was sentenced to 361 days of probation. An earlier case of domestic battery was dropped when Leanne refused to testify, court records showed.

The good life was nothing alien to either of the Paulsens. A native of Alabama, Leanne Serrano Blanton Paulsen, married once before, was a Carmel High School homecoming queen and a 1989 honor student graduate from Indiana University. At Carmel High School, she and her three sisters were all performers. Leanne was in the high school production of *Bye, Bye Birdie* and was a member of the school's show choir and dance group. At IU, Leanne was a member of the Red Steppers Dance Team. In Indianapolis, she was successful with the Civic Theatre and the American Cabaret Theatre. In New York, she danced with the New York City Rockettes and joined the Broadway tours of *South Pacific* and *Jesus Christ Superstar*, in which she played Mary Magdalene.

J.J., a New Yorker, wrote for the television programs *Cosby*, *Grace Under Fire* and *In Living Color*, among others. As a writer for the Comedy Central channel, he went to Hollywood, where his TV credits mounted, and he was nominated for an Emmy. He returned to New York, working at the Kaufman Astoria Studios in his native Queens and as writer and director on the *Cosby* series. He and Leanne met through mutual friends in New York and married in November 2003. They came to Carmel from Los Angeles with the desire to raise a child. After the child was born, neighbors said that Leanne walked around the house in T-shirts and jeans and became reclusive whereas once the Paulsens had once hosted housewarming parties.

In December 2006, Leanne's sisters, Sharon Deam and Gerri Schaffer, began trying to reach her but said they got repeated excuses from J.J., who had also acted as if his wife were alive when a friend had visited the home. On April 14, he had asked the friend to take him and his wife to the airport in a couple of days. But on April 16, the friend was told that the trip would be delayed because of "personal problems."

At that time, as police came to learn, Leanne was already dead. On April 17, Sharon Deam's growing suspicions lead her to ask Carmel police to check on the Paulsen home. They found Leanne's body.

Paulsen was charged with the murder of his wife and for leaving his son home alone; the trial was scheduled in Hamilton County Superior Court. But the passage of two years brought police no confession, no murder weapon and no witnesses. In March 2008, the prosecutors offered Paulsen a deal to plead guilty to involuntary manslaughter and also to neglect of a dependent and moving a body from the scene of death.

The agreement incensed domestic violence advocates, but legal experts said that it was the proper move under the circumstances. Paulsen accepted the plea agreement. On Friday, March 27, he was sentenced to twenty-six years in prison, the maximum.

# Recording of a Murder

Rarely do investigators get as much insight into a slaying as they did in the 1975 murder of Orval Lee Baker, a nineteen-year-old shot on the southwest side of Indianapolis. The suspected killer left a tape recording that contained the sound of the actual murder, a poem describing the flight of a bullet taking a life and a study of assassination. Police had no trouble seizing a suspect.

Neighbors who heard shots called authorities, who found Roger L. Lynn, nineteen, waiting for them at the murder scene—Lynn's home. Lynn was one of Baker's best friends and did not live far from the murder victim. Lynn's arrest on January 24 led to his tape-recorded diary.

"It is bizarre," said deputy prosecutor Christopher Zoeller. "He tells of a fascination with death and says how he is going to kill his friend, then left the tape running during the crime." According to investigators, the day before the slaying Lynn recorded "very deep thoughts." Near the end of the diary was a poem:

*The bullet enters first its chest,*
*Then pierces lungs, heart and breast,*
*The second shot comes thundering through,*
*And brains and skull are thrown astrew,*
*The man lies bleeding and dying,*
*And now there is much crying,*
*Crying of happiness, victory at last,*
*Victory from the second blast.*

It was explained in the diary that the death described in the poem was not a disaster but rather a means of escaping life. Lynn also made a rambling speech in the diary, saying that he would like to be dressed at his funeral in a judo tunic and black, double-knit flared slacks. He also gave some of his views on child rearing. He quoted two Bible verses involving what he termed the power of the grave and destruction. Then Lynn described the slaying, something that stunned the jury at his trial.

*I will now describe a little bit of my plan. I will bring Lee Baker up here and have him look at these books I've got up here—pornographic books, magazines—then while he is looking* [at them] *I will shoot him once in the chest area and once in the head.*

*That will leave me two bullets 'cause I have four bullets in the carbine* [an M-1 carbine, thought to be the murder weapon]. *I will then walk over to the levee, probably the pit, and there will fire one shot into the air, then one shot into my own head.*

The carbine believed used in the slaying had "Nevermore" carved in the stock, a word recurring in Edgar Allen Poe's poem "The Raven."

The tape continued:

*Report, it is 10 minutes after two* [on the day of the slaying]. *Lee* [Baker] *doesn't have to be into work until 4:30. I called up and he is supposed to come down in a few minutes. I will record the entire incident today, and there will be music in the background to hopefully cover up some of the noise, the two shots, so I will leave off now until I resume with the recording of the assassination.*

Lynn recorded a farewell to his wife, Linda, saying, "I'll be alive in mind, in spirit."

The rock-and-roll song "Evil Woman" played loudly on the tape. Then there were the sounds of a shot and a shell casing hitting the floor. About four seconds later, a second shot is heard on the tape. "This is it. I'm sorry, but I have to do this Linda. Goodbye Linda." Then the tape ended.

Investigators claimed that Lynn had been fascinated with the assassinations of President John F. Kennedy, Robert F. Kennedy and Reverend Martin Luther King Jr. He had been chronically truant in school, it was found, and besides watching a lot of television, he had read pornography and works by Poe, a writer known for bizarre writing, often involving savage and peculiar deaths.

Lynn, although admitting to authorities that he had an "urge to kill," pleaded not guilty by reason of insanity. Defense attorneys bolstered their insanity defense by citing evidence that Lynn had once killed a dog just as he had slain Baker. He also had killed another dog, smashed a cat to death against the wall and killed a pet duck.

Would a sane man, asked a defense attorney,

*shave his head three days before the crime; leave a tape recorded diary with thoughts of death; make sexual advances to his mother and grandmother; put mineral oil or castor oil in his grandfather's liquor bottles; try to kill his wife, and even write a confession to the slaying a day before he killed his best friend?*

*When other teen-agers were playing sandlot football and basketball, Roger was in his room reading Edgar Allen Poe, mulling over assassinations and making intricate drawings of the effects of a bullet on the human body. He was writing a diary of how he planned to lure his mother into his bedroom and drawing female bodies—then stuffing the papers into a hole in his bedroom wall.*

However, the Indianapolis jury of nine women and three men found Lynn guilty on September 29, 1976. He was sentenced to life in prison.

Part IV

# By Person or Persons Unknown

Among the most intriguing homicides are those that are unsolved. Sometimes the murderer has never been identified. Sometimes suspects have been tried but acquitted. On rare occasion, a person is convicted of a murder without the identity of the victim being known. Here are some of the city's unsolved, or strangely solved, homicides.

## Not What the Doctor Ordered

It seemed ironic that a prominent thirty-five-year-old female doctor who first introduced a new method for detecting rabies to Indiana should be slain by what appeared to be a "mad dog." Some rejected the killer theory and insisted that the savage slash in her throat must have been self-inflicted. But after intensive investigation, it became clear that neither suicide nor homicide could be entirely supported by the facts, making the death of Dr. Helene Elise Knabe one of the strangest cases in the gallery of unsolved Indianapolis crimes.

Indianapolis detectives, besides lacking a scientific approach to crime in 1911, were tardy in starting on this case. They weren't even told about the bloody corpse until forty-five minutes after it had been found, peered at and touched by at least four people. The police could find no knife, no keys to the apartment, no sign of forced entry and no motives. Some wheel-spinning is understandable. Indianapolis police didn't even have a homicide division for thirty-eight years. DNA was unknown, as were most other investigative tools considered common today.

Helene Knabe is shown in a photo
taken when she was with the
Indiana Board of Health.

The last time Dr. Knabe was seen alive was about 5:00 p.m. on October 23, 1911, when she and her cousin, Miss Augusta Knabe, paused at a downtown streetcar stop after an uneventful day of shopping. "Why don't you come on to my place for a cup of tea?" the doctor asked. Augusta declined.

Returning wearily home, Augusta spent a quiet evening in her flat and retired early. She slept soundly until about 11:30 p.m., when she sat up in her bed, tense with a fear that haunted her for the rest of the night. "I dreamed I was with Dr. Knabe," she told police later, "and that the tail of an enormous black snake hung toward us from a tree. We were speechless with fright, and I felt that we held each other in a close embrace as if every moment would be our last."

Had Augusta arisen and gone to her cousin's ground-floor apartment on the fringe of downtown Indianapolis, she might have arrived in time to prevent Dr. Knabe's death. As it was, it remained for pert, young Miss Katherine McPherson, the doctor's assistant, to saunter into the bloody bedroom at 8:15 the next morning.

The door to the bedroom at the rear of the office was ajar, and a light burned inside. Miss McPherson stepped through the door and froze at a scene she would be asked to describe in minute detail dozens of times in the next few days.

The doctor's right hand, bent upward as if in self-defense, was icy and stiff. The doctor's other arm was extended, and one leg was drawn up slightly at the knee. The doctor was in a pool of half-dried blood. Her head lay back under the iron bed railing, exposing the wound that had cut the jugular vein and nearly severed the windpipe. Miss McPherson, who had some medical indoctrination, didn't act on Dr. Knabe's death, but rather on the possibility of saving her life, she said. "For some reason, I got the idea into my head that Dr. Knabe might still be alive," she was to explain.

Miss McPherson telephoned Public School No. 33, where Augusta taught the German language. Augusta agreed to come at once. Then Miss McPherson began calling doctors she knew. Dr. Frank B. Wynn was not at home, but his wife, who knew Dr. Knabe, said she would stop at the office. Next called was Dr. Ernest C. Reyer, and although he said he would come at once, Miss McPherson also phoned Dr. Charles E. Ferguson and seven other physicians and friends of Dr. Knabe's. Augusta arrived before the doctors.

"Oh, she can't be dead," Augusta cried, covering Dr. Knabe's tummy with a pillow. When the doorbell rang, Augusta answered it and took a fistful of letters from the mailman, making no move to stop him or ask his help.

Dr. Reyer soon arrived, followed by Dr. Ferguson. "It's a case for the coroner and the police, not a doctor," Reyer said. He called authorities. Ferguson peeked under the bed; the floor was covered with blood, which had soaked through the mattress.

Belatedly, detectives Mullin, Morgan, Stewart and Hall, lead by Captain Crane, tromped onto the scene. They had been driven there by Robert Newby Sr., who lived well into the 1950s and distinctly recalled the case. The policemen noted no signs of a struggle. There was no blood elsewhere in the apartment. In the bathroom, two unsoiled towels hung beside the sink. No fingerprints were found and no evidence of someone entering through a window.

"Then Coroner C.B. Durham came, and while he and the doctors were examining the body, our men fanned out through the apartment and adjoining ones and the basement, checking the dumbwaiter and its shaft, looking everywhere for the murder weapon," Newby recalled. Unbeknownst to them, janitor Jefferson Haynes had already called up the dumbwaiter for the garbage can, and it had been placed in the alley and later hauled away.

Dr. Knabe's clothing was in a neat pile on a chair beside the bed. A shirtwaist was on another chair, a fresh handkerchief tucked in the pocket. The physician's surgical instruments were in order, and her medicine case appeared undisturbed. The telephone, also undisturbed, was on the floor

Robert Newby Sr., who drove the police to Helene Knabe's apartment, lived into the 1950s and recalled the case. *Photo by author.*

within easy reach. The doctor's nightgown was pulled up around her shoulders; there was no indication she had been sexually assaulted.

Durham had labeled the death a murder. But some of the policemen thought it was a case of suicide, although there was no suicide note.

Augusta and Miss McPherson quickly pleaded exhaustion and rejected more questioning at the crime scene. They never were kept apart or grilled separately.

Had Dr. Knabe not bowed out with such violence and intrigue, her death still would have aroused public interest. Only three years earlier, she had resigned as an official of the Indiana Board of Health in charge of the hygiene lab, a post never before held by a woman. While on this job, she traveled to New York and learned how to examine a dog's brain to detect rabies. Dr. Knabe had left the lab job with a Teutonic blast. "They expect an employee in the lab to have a man's brain but be paid a woman's salary," she had complained.

The next year, 1909, she became the only woman in the nation teaching in a veterinary college when the Indiana Veterinary College elected her to the chair of parasitology and hematology. In 1910, she became associate professor of physiology and hygiene in the North American Gymnastic Union and was thinking of turning to gymnastics as a career.

She was born Helene Elise Hermine Knabe at Ruegenwalder-Muende, Germany, on December 22, 1875. She spent her youth near the Baltic Sea and grew to love outdoor sports and nature. She took a natural interest in science, but many German women were not allowed to study medicine.

Augusta had gone to America, planning to stay a year. When she decided to stay longer, Dr. Knabe joined her and studied medicine in the United States. In 1896, she began a medical course at Butler University. Studying under Dr. Wynn, Dr. Knabe gained appointment as curator of the college pathological museum in 1902. Two years later, she got her medical degree and became supervisor of the college lab.

One of her close associates was Dr. William B. Craig, who lived a few blocks from her apartment. He helped get Dr. Knabe named to the faculty. Gossip related that the two had a growing amatory relationship. But if it be love, it did not go smoothly. The two had a heated squabble over lecture scheduling at the college.

Dr. Knabe had friends, mostly other doctors, but also enemies created by her outspokenness, bluntness, forcefulness and talent. One of the latter was Dr. W.T.S. Dodds. After the slaying, he said, "Dr. Knabe was an arrogant, headstrong, merciless woman whose ambition to succeed was such that she did not hesitate to sacrifice anyone to achieve success. During her career with the State Board of Health, Dr. Knabe made herself so disliked she was asked to resign."

To police, the apartment janitor, Haynes, seemed an unlikely suspect. Besides, a fellow employee had found him asleep in a chair by the furnace, as usual, about 10:30 p.m. the night of the crime. After going to bed, Haynes said, he heard a woman's moan and a scream in Dr. Knabe's apartment. "I supposed the doctor had a patient who was in pain, so I went back to sleep," the janitor said.

At least three people who had passed the Knabe apartment or lived nearby told police that they had heard screams or someone running in the alley. None investigated further or called police.

The public became intrigued. Private groups called in private detectives. Some private eyes investigated on their own, seeking prestige by solving the case. Even teachers at Augusta's school talked about hiring a detective. Rewards were offered. Superintendent Hyland, although doubtful, pressed ahead on the murder theory: someone had entered the flat, perhaps seeking treatment, overpowered the doctor and killed her.

Ushers were required at the Alonzo M. Ragsdale mortuary the morning of October 28 to handle the funeral crowd. Detectives mingled with the crowd as Dr. Knabe was buried; they learned nothing.

Hyland finally adopted the suicide theory. "We have been unsuccessful in discovering a motive for the murder," he explained. One minor problem was the unearthing of a letter Dr. Knabe had mailed the day of her death to Dr. Nettie B. Powell at Marion, Indiana. Far from suggesting suicide, the letter asked Dr. Powell to come to Indianapolis soon and stay for a few days. Augusta and Miss McPherson still insisted that it was murder. The murder-suicide debate continued. Some called for the investigation to halt—it was futile and indecent, they said.

Ragsdale, the mortician, who was also to administrate Dr. Knabe's estate, went to the flat to catalogue her belongings. He found a microtome knife, used to slice organisms for study under the microscope, and the missing key to Dr. Knabe's flat. It was on the chiffonier, which had been searched several times, in a dust-covered case under some old papers.

Ragsdale auctioned Dr. Knabe's personal effects in the upstairs room of his mortuary. Women came in droves. The doctor's microscope went for sixty dollars, her books for as much as twenty-five dollars each. Iron bars had been installed on the window of the doctor's old apartment, which had been rented to a medical student and his wife.

The inquest report of Coroner Durham showed that he had found Dr. Knabe's books in order, her practice seemingly sound. She treated many dog bite victims, getting seventy-five to eighty dollars for administering the Pasteur treatment, a method compatible with her introduction of the rabies detection method to Indiana. There had been blood on her upper arms but none on her hands. The throat had been cut from right to left; the doctor was right handed. Durham's deputy, Dr. Ralph Chappell, said that the throat showed two slashes. There also was a gash in her left forearm.

"It is true that the weapon could have been concealed," Durham said, "but I know many of the people who were in the room after the body had been found, and I cannot be convinced that they concealed the knife. It would have been impossible, of course, for the women to have cut such a

This building, also gone now, stood on the corner that was the site of Dr. Helene Knabe's apartment. *Photo by author.*

deep wound in her own throat and then to have arisen from her bed to conceal the knife."

"I do hereby find," concluded Durham, "that said decedent came to her death from hemorrhage and shock following the cutting of her throat at the hands of another person or persons—murder."

Durham's verdict fell on a disinterested public. Many were already forgetting the case—but not the local Council of Women. The members hired private detective H.C. Webster, who started sleuthing on February 11, 1912.

Webster submitted evidence to a grand jury in June 1921; the jury did not act. He was back again in December, and this time the jury handed down indictments for Alonzo Ragsdale and Dr. William Craig, charging him with the killing and Ragsdale with helping him. Both men were freed on bond.

The detective's case was that Dr. Craig had helped Dr. Knabe's career and that they became romantically involved. Dr. Craig found a new sweetheart, Miss Katherine Fleming, who said that she and Dr. Craig had discussed marriage. In Webster's scenario, Dr. Knabe and Dr. Craig had a violent quarrel the Sunday before she was slain. Also, Dr. Craig's housekeeper said that Craig came home very late the night of the slaying, changed all his clothing and left early the next morning.

The trial, moved to Shelbyville, was opened on November 28, 1913. A string of witnesses, many of whose stories of strange events the night of the slaying had appeared in the press, paraded through the witness box. The prosecution rested on Sunday, December 8, 1913. The defense moved for acquittal, contending a motive lacking and no connection shown between Dr. Craig and the crime.

The next day, Judge Alonzo Blair ruled for the acquittal, one of the first times in Indiana that a directed verdict was used in a murder trial. In a fifteen-page statement, the judge explained that "there has been no evidence that the defendant murdered Dr. Knabe." The courtroom crowd cheered. The case against Ragsdale was dismissed.

The horrendous slaying of Dr. Knabe was as much a mystery as ever, and it still is. Some believed that the futile trial resulted from a document the defense attorneys passed around. They said that it was a contract between detective Webster and a clairvoyant in which the private eye offered her $300 to pluck the killers from her crystal ball. In retrospect, perhaps a crystal ball was the only reliable clue in this unsolved Indianapolis crime, which was probably murder but possibly something else.

# The Corpse in the Attic

Sometimes murders go unsolved because the trail had gone cold—especially after twenty years and there's little proof that it was a killing in the first place. That was the dilemma caused by the discovery of Carrie Selvage's body in 1920.

Miss Selvage, forty-three, a 118-pound, wren-like woman, was a member of a prominent Indianapolis family. She had taught for years until she underwent a nervous collapse the last day of school in 1900. For her recuperation, the family engaged a large front room at the old Union

State Hospital, which then was located thirteen blocks north of the Indiana Capitol in Indianapolis. On the morning of March 11, Miss Selvage took a walk in the hospital garden, returned to her room and asked her nurse for a glass of milk. Carrie was seated on her bed, wearing a dark blue wrap, her small, slippered feet barely touching the floor. When the nurse came back with the milk, Miss Selvage was gone.

A routine check of the hospital was fruitless. Personnel on duty swore that neither Selvage, nor anyone else, had been seen leaving. The hospital kept the disappearance quiet for two days, hoping that the missing woman would turn up. When the incident was finally made public, it caused a citywide stir. Circulars offering rewards were distributed. Newspapers urged farmers to check isolated fields for a body. The Indianapolis Water Company drained the canal. Streams were dragged. Clairvoyants across the country contacted the family with suggestions. F.T. Davis, an Indianapolis hypnotist, took a boy under a hypnotic spell to Selvage's room. Nothing came of it.

This was the building where the skeleton of Carrie Selvage was found after twenty years. Indianapolis Star *files*.

In 1902, police captured grave robbers who supplied medical schools with cadavers. The leader, Rufus Cantrell, said that he had buried Miss Selvage in a cellar near the hospital, but the cellar yielded nothing. In 1915, a gang seized in Detroit gave similar grave robbing stories. This led to opening graves around Flackville, an Indianapolis neighborhood, as well as Nora and McCordsville. No Carrie.

Then, in April 26, 1920, workman Dan Jones tore open the roof of a building being remodeled on the old Union Hospital site. He saw a skeleton seated on the tin roof of a double attic. Police deduced little until a neighbor with a memory for history suggested contacting the Selvage family.

Joseph Selvage and his brother, Edward, came to the scene. After examining the surviving clothing, they concluded that it was their sister Carrie. A coroner's investigation put it down as death by unknown means. But the brothers believed that Carrie had been murdered.

They pointed out that the skeleton had been seated—not a likely position for someone dying of starvation. Also, the hospital searches had come very close to the attic without hearing any outcries. Thirdly, the searchers had not found the hidden attic, making it unlikely that Carrie could have discovered it; besides, she had poor eyesight. Persons living in the rooming house that replaced the hospital had never found the hidden attic. Someone, the brothers contended, had known about the attic and either lured Carrie there or used it to hide a homicide.

Officials were unmoved. Even if the contention of the brothers were accepted, there was little likelihood of determining after twenty years who had killed Carrie Selvage, if in fact she had been murdered. Today, of course, the buildings from that era have disappeared just as completely as Carrie did.

# After the Race

Even in 1930, there was a lot of traffic after the Memorial Day race at the Indianapolis Motor Speedway. But what attracted the attention of a young man from Clayton, Indiana, who was driving near the Speedway, was the fact that a parked automobile was engulfed in flames.

It was shortly after midnight when the Clayton youth and his companion, an Indianapolis girl, traveling on Rockville Road, saw flames turn the sky red about a quarter-mile away on High School Road. The automobile, seemingly a 1928 Plymouth, was so fiery that it couldn't be approached. The pair did not suspect that anyone was in the vehicle.

Unable, or unwilling, to find a telephone at once and lacking a sense of urgency, the pair continued toward Indianapolis. About a mile later, a man on foot hailed them. He had dark hair and a pockmarked face and requested a ride into town. No, he said, he hadn't seen any car on fire.

The stranger got out in downtown Indianapolis. Then the man from Clayton reported the burning car, and firemen rushed to the scene. It was 1:30 a.m. on May 31 before they reached the vehicle, its Alabama license plate still visible.

When the flames were extinguished, a form was discerned in the front passenger seat. The arms and legs had been destroyed. Identification seemed impossible. But the pocket of a coat found on the grass nearby revealed a wallet containing a premium payment on a $10,000 life insurance policy. It insured Harold Herbert Schroeder, the same name found on an ID card in the wallet.

Examination revealed a wound in a lung of the burned torso, possibly made by an ice pick. Dr. Lawrence Lewis declared that the person, whoever it was, had been murdered. Dr. C.H. Keever, coroner, agreed; a bullet or stab was likely the source of the wound. But who was the victim?

Authorities were suspicious. The car did not appear to have been wrecked; it was carefully parked. The coat, wallet and insurance receipt looked as if they had been planted. Alabama authorities confirmed that the car was registered to Schroeder, who manufactured automobile radiators.

A couple days later, a raincoat was found atop a pile of junk on West Pearl Street. It bore the initials "HHS" on the back. Investigators found witnesses who had watched Billy Arnold win the 500 Mile Race and also had seen a man in the crowd wearing such a raincoat.

They described him as well built and said that he had stood atop his car to get a better view of the race. The name Harold Herbert Schrocder matched the initials. But the burned corpse in the car was not a well-built man. The hitchhiker who had been given a ride into Indianapolis by the young couple matched much better.

When investigation showed that there was a Schroeder living in Mobile, whose wife said he was away on one of his frequent trips, authorities headed for Alabama. Mrs. Schroeder doubted that her husband was dead. She made no plans to collect his $35,000 in insurance. But it was learned that she had received mail from her husband that was postmarked from Indianapolis and Nashville, Tennessee, bearing dates after the car had burned.

The Mobile trip also uncovered a girlfriend of Schroeder's, of whom his wife and two children knew nothing. The paramour said that Schroeder, who had seemed worried, had talked of insurance that would send his boys to college.

Fate stepped in when the Marion County sheriff and his traveling companions bought a newspaper on June 21 at Birmingham, Alabama, as they stopped for lunch. They were on their way back to Indianapolis. The paper the sheriff purchased was headlined "Schroeder Found in Mobile."

Sure enough, Schroeder had been dragged from hiding in some high weeds near his home. Schroeder told the sheriff, "Nuts! You guys got me wrong. I never killed that man."

He stuck to that part of his story. But after being jailed, he told an incredible saga. He was returning after the race to Mobile via St. Louis when he picked up a hitchhiker, a lad twenty-five or thirty years old, who said that he lived in Massachusetts. The hitchhiker fell asleep near Terre Haute. Soon, Schroeder said, he also dozed off and ran into a ditch. "I found the boy evidently had broken his neck. He was asleep in the front seat and his head apparently had hit the dashboard," Schroeder confessed.

For some reason, he drove back to Indianapolis, and for another inexplicable reason, he stopped and set the car afire. "I do not know why," he said. "I was afraid I would be accused of killing this man." He caught the ride with the couple and then hitchhiked to Mobile, he told police. Efforts to shake his confession were futile, even when authorities took him to the mortuary where the body of the fire victim was held, in a crude coffin. As to the puncture wound, said Schroeder, "I don't know who did it."

In Marion County Criminal Court, Schroeder, the model of propriety, using manners he had polished under U.S. Air Force discipline, was convicted, despite the efforts of a spectacular criminal lawyer of that era, Ira Holmes. Schroeder did not take the stand. The jury took three hours and thirty-five minutes to find Schroeder guilty of voluntary manslaughter; the sentence was two to twenty-one years.

For decades, letters reached the sheriff and prosecutor seeking identification of the hitchhiker, many including pictures. Schroeder refused to look at them. "I wouldn't know him," he said.

He was paroled on March 29, 1934, after a trifle more than three years behind bars. He left for parts unknown and was never heard from again in Indianapolis.

A county grave in Floral Park Cemetery was the final resting place of the hitchhiker who met death, whether by accident or by Schroeder's hand. To this day, no one knows whose body was cremated in the Plymouth from Mobile.

# Cash May Have Been the Object

Indianapolis resident Theodore R. Turner was a self-made man who started a string of four gasoline filling stations in the city and thereby grew wealthy. That may have killed him.

About 10:45 p.m. on November 17, 1957, Turner, fifty-one years old, entered the driveway of his home on North Pennsylvania Street. Six shots shattered the quiet of the night. Four of the bullets, which had come from a .45-caliber weapon, entered his chest at close range. Two of the shots passed through his clothing and lodged in the home of a neighbor.

The shots were heard by Turner's daughter Celia, twenty-one, but she thought that perhaps someone was shooting dogs, she later told police. She had been out on a date and got home about 10:20 p.m., not long before her father's fatal arrival, and was reading. About the same time she heard the shots, the Turner dog made a sound as if injured and then began barking. Celia went downstairs, but her examination of the area through a window showed that everything was calm, except for the dog. The daughter returned upstairs and awakened her forty-three-year-old mother Clara and asked what car her father had driven that night.

It was the green 1955 Ford, Mrs. Turner said. Celia had seen it in the driveway. She tried to get the dog to come inside, but the animal barked insistently; Clara Turner, by now aroused, went outside and found her husband in the driveway. She thought he was still alive, but he wasn't.

The victim was face up on the ground. He wore a brown suit, green shirt and brown shoes, and his hat was near his head. He had not bled greatly. In his hands were the car keys, a flashlight and an inventory sheet. Evidently, Turner had been able to get out of the car and walk to the passenger side before being shot.

Police found the six shell casings on the ground by the body and a .41-caliber derringer under the Ford. That weapon became part of the enduring mystery. The family said that it did not belong to Turner; he was afraid of guns. But others swore that he once had asked how to obtain a gun permit. Was Turner afraid for his life, desiring a gun for protection? Had the weapon, unfired, been dropped in panic by the killers?

One theory was that the killer had a military background. The shot pattern in Turner's body hinted at a professional marksman. Others thought it possible that an amateur had acquired a .45-caliber weapon, possibly had stolen it, and it "got away from him" when he opened fire, accounting for the six shots that were strewn across Turner's body from left to right.

## n Was Shot
## le His Home

:ommitted here in recent months re-
rday The Indianapolis Times reviewed
i of Mrs. Malvina Krutz; today, Theo-
v, Dave Miller.

r R. K. SHULL

THE Nov. 17 slaying of oil com-
dore R. Turner immediately brings
irn phrases as "police baffled" and
."

erdict in the case is succinct in
its of nearly four months of police
by person or persons unknown

n be added, but the basic facts
was gunned down in the drive-
is North Side home for reasons
iller with a weapon which may

ently had hid in ambush waiting
i executive to return home on that

, 1957, had been spent by Mr. Turner
ner as other Sundays. Sunday, to Mr.
ir day in his work week which con-
r days," according to his 43-year-old

ide man who had gained substantial
nd-tumble gasoline business here by
oline to the four independent oil sta-

Theodore R. Turner          Mrs. Clara Turner

MURDER SCENE—The "X" marks the spot where Theodore
Turner was found shot to death. The garage door had been
partially raised by the killer who waited inside the garage for
Mr. Turner to arrive home.

is own
is own
: duty
in his
n Nov.

r, Mrs.
ed him
ons at
s. But
ier and

their small dog was in the
backyard, she said.
  As Miss Turner related
events to the coroner's stenog-
rapher the following morning:
  "About 10:45 p. m. I heard
a commotion in the driveway,
but at the time I didn't know
whether it was in our or the

breakfast room window and
did not see anyone. But the
dog was still making a noise.
We then went to the back
door. The dog would not come
in and he was acting as if
she should come out and look,"
Miss Turner said.
  "When mother went out, she

Newspaper details showed the victim and scene where Theodore Turner was killed.
Indianapolis Times files.

A bag with $123 was found on the front floor of the car, and Turner still
had $83 in his wallet. The money in the bag was in the small amounts he
regularly collected from service stations. The major portion of the collection
was routinely put in a bank depository, the family said. The bank later
confirmed that Turner had made the deposit that fateful night. Police came
to believe that the gunmen knew of his collection routine, waited for him

and, when they found most of the money had been banked, panicked, shot him and fled without taking the amount Turner had in his possession.

Mrs. Turner had accompanied her husband when he collected from two of his four filling stations earlier that Sunday, but had become ill, returned home and went to bed. Turner, who as a precaution never collected twice in the same family car, had left the two Cadillacs in the garage. Returning home, Turner had to go down a 150-foot driveway and open the gate in a spiked iron fence to get to the garage. The fence gate was still agape when police arrived, and the garage door was open about three feet. One theory was that the killer or killers had waited inside the garage.

Neighbors had not seen anyone flee the scene, but police found evidence of flight though the rear of the property—evidently someone climbed atop a picnic table and scaled the tall fence at the rear.

Turner had started his filling stations several years earlier. Although he had become wealthy, he still did his own collecting and bookkeeping. Some suggested that his slaying wasn't about cash at all, but rather involved competition with oil firm executives or was related to hot market gasoline sales.

Police also considered that the Turner murder might have been linked to the robbery on Saturday, November 2, of Sol J. Solomon, president of a butcher company. Solomon was slugged and robbed by a masked hoodlum who leaped out of the bushes as Solomon neared his home, less than a dozen blocks from the Turner residence.

Ten days after Turner was murdered, police thought that they had a break. Among fingerprints taken at burglary sites on the north side of Indianapolis was one print that led them to 230-pound John Alfred Williams. The suspect was nabbed without a struggle. He confessed to four burglaries but denied the Turner killing; a lie detector test cleared him.

Hope arose again in 1963. Police announced that they had recovered a government-issued .45-caliber weapon, found in front of a house near the Turner home. The weapon, rusty and evidently left outside for some time, was discovered by a ten-year-old boy. The serial numbers were sent to the Federal Bureau of Investigation (FBI) in the hope, which proved futile, that ownership could be established.

To this day, the Turner murder is unsolved—no clues at the scene, no clear-cut motive and no witnesses. The slaying remains as puzzling as the bouncing prices of gasoline. And still a mystery is why the Turner dog remained quiet until after his master had been murdered.

# Bathroom Brutality

When Malvina Krutz's husband returned home on January 29, 1958, he found his wife in the bathtub. But she wasn't soaking in hot water to ward off the Wednesday chill. In fact, the water was lukewarm. The forty-one-year-old woman had been beaten and drowned. Her five-foot, six-inch, 145-pound body was still partly clothed. There seemed to be little logical reason for the slaying.

The Krutzes' two-bedroom home was in a fairly stable and upscale area on Guilford Street in Broad Ripple. Her husband Charles—at forty-eight, eight years older than his wife—had a stable job as a sales manager for a transportation company in town; he had arrived home in the company car, a red and white Ford.

Investigation revealed that the Krutzes' son, Charles "Bud," had come home from school for lunch and had out-of-sight conversations with his mother, who was in the bathroom and said she was ill. This had happened before, the ten-year-old told police. When Bud arrived after school, Malvina's 1955 Buick was gone, but the boy thought she was delivering his newspapers, as she had said she would, or was visiting friends. The lad was watching *Wild Bill Hickok* on television when his father arrived home.

The boy commented that his bedroom was a mess—"I don't like the looks of it." Charles Sr. went to the bathroom to wash his hands, pulled back the bathtub's shower curtain and found his wife dead. When he called police, it was 5:11 p.m.

Malvina was on her right side, her face up and angled toward the faucet. She wore a brassier and a white blouse, a white cardigan sweater (buttons in the front, with only the top button fastened) and mukluk-like footies. Her panties were rolled down in the back halfway to the knees. Crumpled under her right shoulder and head were a rubber bath mat, a bath rug and a washcloth. She had bruises on the chin and around the left eye. There was blood in her mouth. Later examination revealed that she had been stuck with a fist hard enough to cause a hemorrhage at the rear of the brain, but the bleeding was not fatal. The drowning was.

In the boy's disarrayed room were Malvina's red and green toreador pants, ripped and wet. Bed covers were pulled back, and two pillows on the floor bore spots of blood. A pencil had strands of Mrs. Krutz's hair; she often stuck a pencil in the bun of her dark brown tresses. There was money in the house. It appeared that the woman had been dragged at some point, but she evidently had not been raped. There was no accurate estimate of time of death.

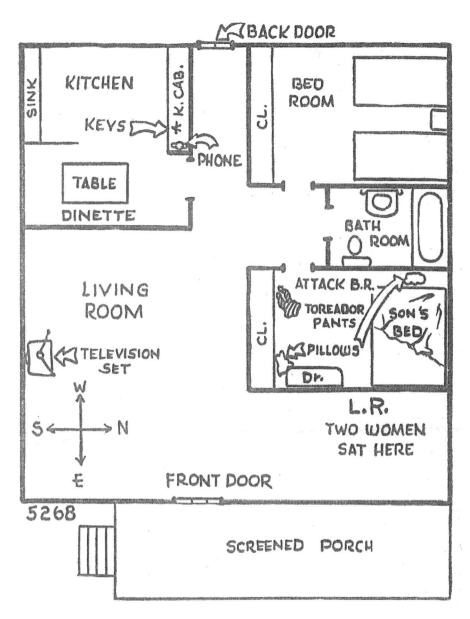

A schematic of the Krutz home showed elements of the bathtub murder of Malvina.
Indianapolis Times *files*.

What developed in the investigation was how closely several people had come to the moment of death. The milkman arrived at the rear door and asked Bud, who was eating his lunch, what to leave. The boy left, returned and said to continue the regular delivery.

A friend of the Krutz couple, Mrs. Mildred Warner, had telephoned the house about 12:45 p.m. on the day of the murder. A shopping trip for wallpaper had been planned. A man had answered the phone. The caller could not identify him. Through him, Mrs. Warner relayed the message that she had a ride. The caller definitely said that she had heard Malvina's voice. Later, Warner arrived at the Krutz house with Mrs. Florence Cubert. They had to stop to let Malvina's car exit the driveway. They did not see who was driving, except that it was a man wearing a hat. Had they seen the killer? A neighbor boy also witnessed the car being driven away.

Getting no answer to knocks, Warner and Cubert entered the Krutz house through the kitchen door, found the bedroom doors closed and actually waited ten or fifteen minutes in the living room, evidently assuming the Malvina was dressing for their outing. Had Malvina already been killed at that time? The pair left a note and departed.

Police had verified Charles Krutz's afternoon sales calls, and he also passed two lie detector tests. Although Krutz insisted that all was well in the marriage, Malvina had filed for divorce on January 13, charging her husband with neglect of his conjugal duties. She was seeing a psychiatrist and a medical doctor; she had a slipped disc and a thyroid condition. A court hearing on the divorce was scheduled for the day after the murder.

Malvina's 1955 Buick automobile, minus its ignition keys, was found about 8:30 a.m. the next morning, eleven blocks from the house. Police first focused on repairmen. A fire at the Krutz home on December 13 had damaged the kitchen and main bedroom. Since then, at least twelve repairmen had been in the home. A carpenter who had been in the Krutz home shortly before the killing was questioned but cleared. Similarly, a thirty-seven-year-old house painter who had worked at the Krutz home was grilled for days. Police considered him a suspect but could not link him directly to the crime.

The painter, Leroy Penick, later was linked to a different crime, tried and convicted. He was sentenced in 1963 for the March 10, 1962 fatal beating of his common-law wife, Carole Jean Martin. Police had, of course, found Penick's fingerprints in the Krutz house.

The *Indianapolis Star* had offered a $5,000 reward for a tip leading in the case, and many were received before the May deadline. One, marked "5000" by the newspaper, was given to police and turned up in December 1960, two and a half years after the slaying. Investigators had never checked out the information; the tip somehow was misplaced.

The letter writer said that he was passing an intersection only a few blocks from the Krutz house on the day of the slaying and saw a man leaving a car on Meridian Street, the main north–south street in Indianapolis and the street where the Krutz car had been found. "He ran like a speed racer south on Meridian," the writer continued, "just as light was changing. While crossing the street he made a movement towards his cap (painter's type) but seemed to toss something toward the west."

Later, the tipster said, he was passing the same area and saw boys pick up something and heard them say that somebody evidently had lost their car keys. The letter writer described the man he saw as very dark-complexioned and having a mustache. Another witness, who had seen the Krutz car being driven away from the house, described the operator as an African American.

Police urged the letter writer to contact authorities, but nothing came of it. The tipster's identity remains as mysterious as the identity of Malvina Krutz's killer.

# Bloodbath for Three

Few homicides in Indianapolis have been as dramatic and puzzling as the slaying of three business partners in December 1971 on LaSalle Street. During forty-five consecutive days of investigation, a team of detectives questioned hundreds of persons, including 180 associates or customers of the slain men and gave lie detector tests to nearly 50 people. The LaSalle Street homicides were at one time or another linked to three other Indianapolis area killings and sometimes were linked to organized crime. Once, a suspect was indicted by the grand jury, but the case was so weak that he was released on bond; the case later was dismissed, and he threatened to sue the Indianapolis Police Department.

To this day, the slayings are unsolved, although one major suspect was "exonerated" by dying.

It was a chilly Wednesday night on December 1, 1971, when John Karnes went hunting for his friends at the home they occupied on LaSalle Street on the east side of Indianapolis. He had missed connecting with them in calls to their office, where their secretary expressed concern that they had not returned to work. When Karnes approached the house, he found the front door ajar. He entered and discovered a bloodbath.

When he called police from a nearby telephone, his report that "there's been a triple murder" was doubted at first. But after Patrolman Michael D. Williams determined that Karnes evidently had made a legitimate report, the officer accompanied Karnes into the house at 1318 North LaSalle Street. When Williams saw the crime scene, he hurriedly called for every investigative aide available to Indianapolis police.

Three men were dead—later identified as Robert Gierse, thirty-five; Robert W. Hinson Jr., twenty-seven; and James C. Barker, twenty-six. They had been bound hand and foot and their throats slashed with a sharp instrument that cut almost to the spinal cord. Each was in a different room in the house: Gierse in his own back bedroom, hands and feet bound with sheets and gagged with a piece of shirt; Hinson in his bedroom, struck three times and, like Gierse, gagged with a piece of shirt and bound with sheets and cord; and Barker in the bathroom that was located between the two bedrooms, his ankles tied with pieces of sheets and his wrists tied with a cord, and he was also gagged with a piece of sheet. The police department's new videotape machine recorded every detail, the first time it had been used in a murder case. The entire house was dusted for fingerprints, but all of them were identified as those of the victims or their friends.

The coroner said indications were that each victim had been held by the hair while their throats were cut. Each also had been struck on the head. A robbery motive was ruled out; all of the victims had money in their pockets. A solitary killer seemed unlikely to investigators; the three men were large, all more than six feet tall and each was well built and weighed more than two hundred pounds. They worked out at a health club in Indianapolis. The murder scene showed only one sign of struggle—Gierse had a slash on his arm.

At first blush, police only learned that Hinson and Gierse, both bachelors, had recently formed B&B Microfilm Service Company on East Tenth Street. Their microfilming would later become part of a theory of the crime. Baker, who had formerly lived at the LaSalle Street address, was an employee of a camera company. Karnes had visited B&B at about 2:00 p.m. the day of the slaying to talk to Hinson and Gierse when secretary Mrs. J.T. Cole expressed concern.

Mrs. Cole, who lived on the east side of Indianapolis, had worked for six years with the men at Records Security Corporation near downtown before the men started their own business in mid-November. Barker, she said, also had worked at Records Security. On Tuesday, Mrs. Cole said, Hinson and Gierse said they planned to go home about 6:00 p.m. and return to work later.

The LaSalle Street victims and the location where their bodies were found were shown in newspapers after the murder. Indianapolis Star *files.*

A neighbor reported seeing a yellow Oldsmobile across from the LaSalle Street house from 7:00 p.m. to 9:00 p.m. on Monday. It contained two men. Another neighbor later reported a dirty cream-colored car containing three men parked across from the house on the night before the murders. Police had answered a run to the address on the Sunday before the murders and found a woman crying in a car. She said she was a girlfriend of one of the men and had fought with him. Police left after making sure she was all right.

By Friday, police had developed a theory about the slayings. Gierse had probably arrived home first. He had only time to doff his overcoat before being killed. He was wearing dark gray trousers, a red shirt with pale white stripes and black shoes and socks, the same garb he had worn to work that day. His overcoat was hanging in the hall closet. The other two men were seized, bludgeoned and killed immediately after entering the house, police believed. Hinson was fully clothed, the same garb he had worn to work. Barker was fully clothed except for a missing shoe. Cars of all three victims were found parked nearby.

On Friday, Mrs. Cole received four threatening telephone calls. Police protection was provided for her.

By December 6, police were investigating the theory that B&B, the firm named using the first names of Bob Gierse and Bobby Hinson, might be pivotal in finding a motive. One theory was that Gierse had borrowed money from loan sharks to set up the firm and had failed or refused to pay up. Another possibility was that the men had microfilmed sensitive material and were killed to forestall them passing on information about it. Reportedly the men had microfilmed material for banks, the Pentagon, the FBI and the Central Intelligence Agency (CIA). Some microfilm was missing from the house, police said.

Another possibility was that organized crime, which was trying to infiltrate the microfilming business, had slain the trio or ordered them killed to silence them or to provide a warning to others. Boxes of records filled the garage behind the LaSalle Street house, and more records were found in a garage behind the B&B business. Other possible motives were that a large insurance policy on Robert Gierse might have been involved or that the trio had been slain by jealous lovers or husbands. The men, it was learned, had conducted contests to see which of them could seduce the most women.

Gierse, who owned the house, had met the famed Teamster boss Jimmy Hoffa in 1966 and also had worked for Senator Charles Percy of Chicago, as well as other GOP election groups. One of Percy's twin daughters had been murdered in 1967. Police wondered if there was a connection.

This home, site of the LaSalle Street slayings, has been modified from that time and bears a "no trespassing" sign. *Photo by author.*

Soon other possible connections—and murders—surfaced. John C. Terhorst, twenty-five, had been slain via two bullets to the head. His body had been found on March 8, 1971, in Eagle Creek near Zionsville. Terhorst, an Indianapolis microfilm salesman, was known to Hinson and Gierse; police had questioned them about Terhorst's death. Terhorst, police said, had gotten a call from a "Bobby," causing police to wonder if the caller was Robert Hinson. Terhorst had gone to a nearby east-side neighborhood to see a person who expressed interested in Terhorst's 1966 black Corvette. The Corvette never was found.

Police also wondered if the slaying of convicted burglar Bobby Lee Atkinson was linked to the LaSalle Street killings. Atkinson had been slain much like Terhorst had been. Atkinson's body had been found on October 9, 1971, in a lover's lane east of Brooklyn in Morgan County. He, like Terhorst, had been shot twice in the head with a small-caliber pistol. Police believed that Atkinson, who had been convicted of burglary, was still committing burglaries. A stolen typewriter had been found at B&B. Authorities speculated that Atkinson might have been a link between organized crime and the LaSalle Street victims.

A newspaper montage gave details of the LaSalle Street killings, still a mystery. *Indianapolis Star files.*

On December 11, 1971, while police still struggled to find clues in the LaSalle Street slayings, the body of a woman was found in Hancock County. She had been shot three times in the back of the head with a .38-caliber weapon. Although the body was almost skeletal, pathologists suggested that she might have been Mrs. Susan K. Dancer, twenty-four, who had been reported missing in June 1971. Clothing on the skeleton matched those Dancer was wearing when she was last seen. Police said that the slayings of Terhorst, Atkinson and Dancer, if the body was really her, were all conducted in what they called "gangland style."

There was speculation in the press that Indianapolis policemen might be dragging their feet on solving the LaSalle Street slayings because of friendship with a local figure associated with organized crime. Beyond that, some thought that the use of many policemen and the conducting of numerous interviews had scattered the investigation. Policemen pressed into service did not always have an overview of the case or knew what angles were important. As a result, some tips were not pursued and some interviews were not recorded. Some interviews were never conducted, and some interviewees reported that police had done little to follow up on information provided.

Concentration on the sexual activities of the victims and the theory that spurned lovers or jealous husbands might be involved seemed to have led nowhere. The investigators learned that Barker was leading in the contest as to which of the three could seduce the most women. The tally for the year up to the murders was twenty-five for Barker, twenty for Gierse and eighteen for Hinson, police reported.

In the end, the case became one without murder weapons, known witnesses or substantial clues. Many believed the killer or killers were professionals, cunning amateurs or simply lucky in leaving few traces.

After twenty years, police were led to a former mechanic from Mars Hill on the west side of Indianapolis who was serving time in Florida for murder. The mechanic, Floyd M. Chastain, said that he, Carroll Horton and a third man, then deceased, had participated in the slayings. Horton was indicted in March 1996. Chastain was brought from Florida to testify. He claimed that President Richard Nixon and imprisoned Teamster president Jimmy Hoffa (whom Gierse had met in 1966) had masterminded the murders. Chastain also admitted that he had lied. He testified, in fact, that he had given at least five versions of the crime.

Investigators said that their main suspect had never been Horton. They had been interested in the late Jasper, Indiana owner of a microfilm business who once had employed Gierse and Hinton. The Jasper connection, while alive, told investigators that he had talked to Gierse and Hinson on Tuesday, November 30, but didn't know if they had answered at the office or at the LaSalle Street house; the telephone rang at both sites.

Horton was freed after the prosecutor declared that the charges could not be successfully pursued. Charges against Chastain were dropped.

The LaSalle Street house later reverted to the mortgage company. Today, the violent slayings there remain as much a mystery as ever, perhaps unsolved because there were just too many possible motives, too many investigators involved and too many possible suspects.

# Making a Killing in the Restaurant Business

Nobody can really say what happened at the Burger Chef in Speedway, in west-side Indianapolis, on the early morning of November 18, 1978. Only the killer or killers survived, and they haven't talked. What's known is solely that four young employees were abducted, taken to a field in Johnson County and stabbed, beaten and shot.

There was some $500 taken from the Burger Chef safe. Authorities thought possibly that a robbery had gone bad and that perhaps one of the employees recognized the holdup men; all may have been killed to foil identification. But other theories arose during the subsequent dead-end investigation, including angry reaction to a drug debt. It was suggested that the "robbery," in which some money was left behind, had been staged to conceal the real aim of the homicides.

The only sure thing was that four had been murdered: Jayne C. Friedt, twenty years old, assistant manager of the restaurant; Ruth E. Shelton, seventeen, a junior at Northwest High School in Indianapolis; Daniel R. Davis, sixteen, a junior at Decatur Central High School, Indianapolis; and Mark S. Flemmonds, sixteen, a sophomore at Speedway High School. Their slayings occurred along a private drive in a hilly area about a mile east of Indiana 37 in Johnson County. It was later determined that Friedt had been stabbed to death (a knife was still in her body), Flemmonds had been beaten to death and Davis and Shelton were shot to death with a pistol or rifle, possibly when they tried to flee. Their bodies were found on November 19, two days after their disappearance from the Speedway restaurant, by the property owner.

What was the Speedway Burger Chef in November 1978 has today become a financial site. *Photo by author.*

Nothing was found in the backgrounds of the victims to suggest criminal connections. In the weeks before this crime, Speedway had experienced bombings and the murder of a female resident. The additional quadruple slayings stirred community anxiety. The investigation established the following scenario.

The Burger Chef employees were going about closing duties. The restaurant closed at 11:00 p.m. and cleanup usually took two hours. One worker brought doughnuts for all to share from a shop next door. Evidently, they were taking out the trash bags when the abduction occurred. Fellow employee Brian Kring, seventeen, stopped by to visit one of the workers. He discovered the back door, usually kept locked, standing open about three inches. He went inside, found the Burger Chef deserted and the safe in the manager's office open. Purses belonging to Friedt and Shelton were in the restaurant. Several rolls of change were in the safe.

It was not known how the abducted quartet was taken to Johnson County, but Friedt's car was found later that Saturday parked in Speedway. When the bodies were discovered in the wilderness area, nearby residents, some of whom had upscale homes, could offer no clues.

Burger Chef Systems Inc. offered a $25,000 reward. The *Indianapolis Star* offered to receive anonymous letters offering clues; the letters would be numbered. Composite photos of two men who had been seen in the restaurant parking lot were circulated, and soon clay busts were made using the photos as guides.

State police, joined by Indianapolis police and Speedway police in the investigation, put three men under suspicion because they had robbed fast-food restaurants. No arrests were made. A man arrested in Oklahoma for mass murders had been in Speedway the night of the abductions. He was eliminated as a suspect. Checks with Cincinnati, Milwaukee and Kilgore, Texas suspects lead nowhere.

In April 1980, a man who had once been a suspect was arrested for robberies of fast-food outlets elsewhere, but he was cleared. The murder of three employees at a bowling alley in Houston, Texas, bore similarities to the Speedway crime, but no connection was established. James Friedt, brother of the victim, was seized for delivery of cocaine, but he was cleared of any part in the murders. Kevin M. Flemmonds, brother of one victim, was seized for another slaying in Indianapolis but was not linked to the Speedway killings. By late in 1983, most good leads had dissipated.

In 1986, a man in prison for other offenses suggested in letters to the newspapers and subsequent interviews that he knew something about the

A door ajar here at the rear of the Burger Chef led to discovery of the abductions and murders. *Photo by author.*

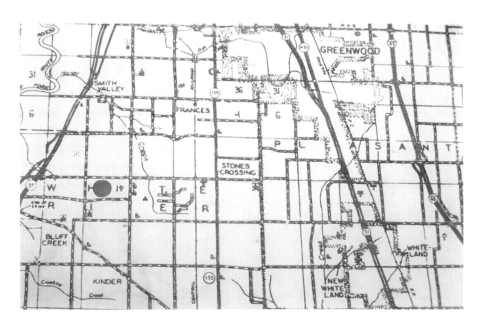

The dot shows the approximate location in Johnson County where bodies of the Burger Chef victims were found. *Map by author.*

Burger Chef killings. He had served a term of five years after pleading guilty to a rape. He was later charged with the rape and abduction of another woman, who feared for her life, and he got a ninety-five-year sentence.

Brought to Indianapolis, this man took police to a yard in Speedway where he said evidence was buried. Digging revealed nothing. He also produced cartridge shells that he said were from the scene of the killing. His refusal to go further and name names was prompted, he said, because if the killers knew he had talked, they would murder him, even though he was in prison. His assistance resulted in nothing.

In the end, although police had some viable suspects and had even received aid from Indianapolis psychics, the murder of the four Burger Chef employees had to be listed as unsolved. The slayings were the more tragic because they snuffed out the lives of four young people who seemingly were leading productive lives and whose future was cut short in rural Johnson County.

# No Bone Unturned

In 1994, a youngster named Erich Baumeister found a skull on his family's property in Hamilton County. Then other bones of a skeleton were discovered. Erich's mother, Juliana, was a little startled but accepted the story of her husband Herb Baumeister, Erich's father, that the skeleton was left over from his father's medical career.

Herb's father had, in fact, been a doctor, and Herb had a quick and easy way of explaining unusual occurrences. Besides, Juliana had grown accustomed to their strange lifestyle and Herb's tendencies to be controlling and a perfectionist. It was not until later that the skull took on different, macabre meaning. Then even Juliana, who claimed ignorance of her husband's later-revealed double life, had to acknowledge that no skeleton from a medical school was involved in the incident at the Baumeister farm.

To this day, there is little certainty about the Baumeister case, except that Herb killed himself before authorities could question him about the eerie discoveries at the eighteen-acre Fox Hollow Farm near 157th Street far north of Indianapolis. Some authorities were convinced that Baumeister was a serial killer, one of Indiana's most prolific, and possibly an Ohio killer as well. Others were unconvinced. One reason is that although parts of seven to ten bodies were unearthed at Fox Hollow Farm, no head was ever discovered and no specific causes of the deaths could be established from the bones.

When the cache of bones was uncovered, investigators hoped that they would provide a link to the ten gay Indianapolis men who had been reported missing between April 1993 and August 1995. One of them, Jeff Jones, was last seen outside the Salvation Army Detox Center in Indianapolis, where he had been dropped off to get help for his drinking. He had worked for a catering company that was said to be a front for gay prostitution. Pictures of another, Roger Alan Goodlet, were posted in some of the Indianapolis gay bars. He was mildly retarded, drank a lot, frequented gay bars and had been arrested a few times. His mother, who spearheaded a search for him, told police that Roger did not realize he was doing anything wrong. Names of a few other missing gay men surfaced. Some weren't identified at all; often their families did not know where they were or what they were doing.

Baumeister took anything he knew about the missing gay men—and most investigators are convinced he knew a lot—to the grave when he shot himself in the forehead on July 3, 1996, in Piney Provincial Park, Sarnia, Ontario. He evidently had fled there as police and forensic investigators were sorting through the mind-boggling array of bones and fragments, many of them burned and scattered like leaves around Fox Hollow Farm.

The ensuing probe revealed a startling double life that Baumeister had led. He had associated with numerous gay Indianapolis men. Yet he evidently was a loving and thoughtful father to three children born to him and Juliana.

Where this tale of killing began is difficult to trace. Certainly Baumeister had a history of bizarre behavior. Juliana Saiter Baumeister seemingly accepted it almost from the start of their marriage on November 21, 1971, after they met on the Indiana University Bloomington campus. Baumeister studied anatomy, an ironic subject as it later developed, intending to follow in the footsteps of his father, Herbert E. Baumeister.

Little seemed awry, at least until facts came out later, as the Baumeisters went about their wedded life. They lived in a few places, including a house on Seventy-second Street in Indianapolis. Herb had a rocky career at the Department of Motor Vehicles and worked at an Indianapolis Thrift Store and also at the *Indianapolis Star* newspaper. In 1988, he and Juliana founded Thrift Management Inc. in Indianapolis.

The business seemed a win-win undertaking. The Baumeisters bought and received donations of all kinds of goods, which they sold at Sav-A-Lot stores; a percentage of the proceeds went to the Children's Bureau in Indianapolis. All seemed well. In 1991, despite their tight budget, they were able to buy on contract Fox Hollow near U.S. 31 and Indiana 32, not far from Westfield. It was what might be called a starter mansion, with swimming pool, acreage and woods, somewhat isolated. About the same time, the Sav-A-Lot business began needing rescue.

What Juliana and the three children—Erich, Marne and Emily—did not know was that Baumeister was frequenting gay bars in Indianapolis, many of them near the Indianapolis–Marion County Public Library on St. Claire Street.

The gay association aside, Baumeister engaged in a string of weird events in his life. He was arrested in 1994 for drunk driving at Rochester, Indiana, paid a $150 fine and spent three days in jail. He never told his wife about it. But, she later revealed, Herb was often gone, giving little explanation or calmly dismissing questioning. At one point, his father committed Herb to LaRue Carter Hospital in Indianapolis, an institution that gave relatively short-term treatment for mental illness. Herb was there for about two months.

During a brief job at the Indiana Division of Motor Vehicles when he was a young man, he exhibited such odd behavior that fellow employees later remarked about it to investigators. He cried a lot, his wife said, and often appeared troubled. In 1985, Herb used a friend's car and got into an accident. He was found not guilty at a trial on charges of theft and conspiracy to commit theft.

Juliana revealed during the investigation at the farm that she had never seen Herb naked. Sex between them occurred only a few times, she said. On their wedding night, Herb had brought a magazine to bed, she told police.

The Baumeister murder case developed after a man who met Herb in one of the gay bars accompanied Baumeister to a home far north of Indianapolis one night; Baumeister said that he was housesitting there. It was actually the Fox Hollow Farm. This strange encounter caused Baumeister's spur-of-the-moment companion to later go to Indianapolis authorities and report his suspicions. He asked for anonymity.

The companion said the house was a mess. He came to doubt that Baumeister was housesitting. The pool had mannequins around it. There was a Christmas tree in place, although the holiday was months away. There was a bar, and eerie conversations with Baumeister caused his partner for the night to believe he was in danger. When Baumeister left the next day, the man fled. He said that he suspected that Baumeister had killed a homosexual acquaintance who had disappeared.

The anonymous tipster agreed to alert authorities if Baumeister again showed up in the gay bars. One night, he did. The tipster obtained the license plate number on the truck Baumeister was driving. The truck license turned up documents that gave Baumeister's address as his former house on Seventy-second Street, which he still owned. However, one document made out by employees at Sav-A-Lot gave the Fox Hollow Farm address.

An Indianapolis Police Department detective in missing persons had taken the tipster on trips north of Indianapolis and into Hamilton County, hoping that he could identify the house to which Baumeister had taken him. Private detectives hired by relatives of missing men added their suspicions in the case. With this information, the detective confronted Baumeister and his wife about his life in gay bars. He admitted it. Juliana was incensed. But both denied police the right to search their property.

Authorities called on Dr. Stephen Nawrocki, a forensic pathologist at the University of Indianapolis. Nawrocki and his crew had been involved in making identifications in several high-profile cases in Indianapolis. He checked the Fox Hollow Farm from a helicopter with infrared equipment but uncovered nothing suspicious.

About that time, Baumeister took his son, Erich, to his mother's house on Lake Wawasee. Juliana, evidently upset by the onslaught of new facts about her husband, asked police to force Baumeister to return the boy. They demurred (they had no jurisdiction or evidence of a crime), but Juliana had begun to revise her interpretation of the skull that had been found. She approved a search of the farm. Indianapolis police asked skeptical Hamilton County authorities to join them.

Juliana took the investigators to a spot where burning had taken place near the home patio. Teeth and bones were found. "They were all over the place," said one Hamilton County deputy. The bones were taken to Nawrocki. He found they were human.

On the next day, June 25, 1996, a search warrant was obtained, and Nawrocki and his staff began combing a small area. Bones were everywhere. Animals feeding on the bones, which showed signs of burning, had scattered them.

Authorities searched the house. It was so large and there was so much debris that the search took a full day. Nothing suspicious was found in the dwelling. The same resulted from a search of the house on Seventy-second Street, although it contained a mannequin. The next day, Juliana began to tell police details about the marriage and Herb's habits.

Meanwhile, back at Fox Hollow, Nawrocki and his crew found hyoids, which are small bones that sit above the voice box; their condition suggested strangulation. In two and a half days, the bone search turned up 5,500 bones, teeth and bone fragments. But no skulls.

Fox Hollow neighbors led authorities to a creek bank, where there was a compost pile that bristled with bones. There were human hands, rib cages, mandibles, spinal columns and arms, a total of 140 bones. There was an old pair of handcuffs. Nawrocki, who first had thought that four bodies were involved, raised his estimate to at least seven bodies; he had discovered seven left thumbs. Later, in 1997, Nawrocki found more bones in the creek bed. There were still no skulls, but he increased his body estimate to nine.

Baumeister's suicide halted all definite conclusions about the Fox Hollow Farm bones. He had shot himself in the forehead with a .357 Magnum. He was well dressed and left a two-page suicide note. It said nothing about the bones. "My whole life is falling apart," the note reported. Investigation showed that Baumeister had twice called his brother, Brad, asking for money. It was wired to him both times. Some thought that the suicide was evidence that Baumeister had killed some or all of the missing Indianapolis gay men.

Baumeister quickly came under suspicion as the so-called I-70 killer. Nine gay white men had been found dumped in shallow streams in Indiana and Ohio near the interstate. Some had been strangled; some corpses had handcuffs marks. The first slaying had occurred in 1980, before the Baumeisters acquired the farm. And the so-called I-70 murders stopped in 1990, two days before Herb and his family moved onto Fox Hollow. Dental records had identified some of the slain homosexuals.

Juliana, who had moved with the children back to Seventy-second Street after Fox Hollow Farm reverted to the original Kentucky owners, said that she found unfamiliar clothing in the house. She also found a man's driver's license and a time sheet bearing another man's name. She did not recognize either name.

Then, in June 1983, two boys found a body, partly clothed, in a stream in rural Hancock County. It was identified as that of a twenty-two-year-old laborer named Michael Riley. Investigators learned that Riley had been seen leaving a north-side Indianapolis theatre with a man who looked like Herb Baumeister. A photo showed Riley with another man, identifiable as Herb Baumeister, in part because of a distinctive wristwatch Herb was wearing in the photo.

That was enough for some. Baumeister fit the profile of serial killers— obsessive-compulsive, a detail-oriented planner, a glib person easily able to have a secret life and deflect suspicion.

Juliana wrote about life with Baumeister for an Indianapolis monthly magazine in a story called "The Secret Life of a Serial Killer." Newspapers all over the nation carried the story of the bone-covered farm in Hamilton

County and the slain homosexuals. Many people doubted that Juliana was fooled by her husband's activities in the gay community. Nawrocki, who had numerous conversations with Juliana, said he was convinced that she was unaware of Baumeister's activities. Baumeister, Nawrocki pointed out, was a skillful manipulator and cunning liar. Juliana, according to most evidence, was beguiled by a pleasant home life, had nowhere else to go, doted on her children and accepted tranquility. Until the skull showed up in the yard.

The Hamilton County sheriff's department says the case still is open. Whether Baumeister was the most prolific killer in Indiana history is not convincingly proven. That he was involved with homosexuals who turned up missing seems certain. And the bones at Fox Hollow Farm don't lie, but they don't reveal the entire story. The one man who may have known the total story chose to die with it untold.

# The Body of Evidence

Police and prosecutors had mostly circumstantial evidence, but it was enough. They had the arguments between Steven D. Halcomb and his former wife, Karen Jo Smith. They had letters and statements from prisoners with whom Halcomb had been incarcerated, and they had the statements he had made to his father, Stan. They had evidence that Karen Jo had not used her credit card since disappearing and had not refilled her medical prescriptions. What they didn't have was a body.

Karen Jo and Halcomb were married in 1991 and were divorced three years later, but not before Halcomb was seen stalking his wife at her Indianapolis beauty salon job. He also called her there numerous times; once, one of Karen Jo's coworkers encountered the couple arguing. Halcomb had his hands around Karen Jo's neck and threatened to kill her rather than lose her, the coworker said.

Halcomb's criminal history included convictions for dealing cocaine, dealing marijuana and causing a death while driving drunk. After he was released from prison, he was living with Karen Jo and her two children, although the couple was divorced. On that Christmas day in 2000, the oldest child, Brandon, twelve, saw his mother and stepfather fighting and interceded to stop it.

Two days later, after the thirty-five-year-old-woman had ordered Halcomb out of her home, she disappeared. She left behind her children, Brandon and Stephanie, her car and all her valuables. Also missing were Halcomb and his car. Two years later, a Marion County grand jury called to consider the case brought charges against Halcomb. Prosecuting someone for murder without a victim's body is uncommon. The trial began on December 7, 2004.

Part of it was testimony that Halcomb had tried to hire an undercover policeman to kill his wife. Also found were letters to Karen Jo in which he told her that his research had shown that without a body there was no murder in 99 percent of the cases. In the letters, he also threatened to kill her. Telephone conversations between Halcomb and his father from jail had been recorded. In them, he told his father that investigators were "not going to find a…thing." Fellow inmates testified that Halcomb had told them that he gave his former wife a one-way ride out of Indianapolis and also that he had strangled her. There are always problems with convicts' testimony—sometimes they recant, sometimes their veracity is questioned.

Nevertheless, on December 15, 2004, a jury found Halcomb guilty.

The members of the defense, taking its cue from the lack of a body, had suggested that Karen Jo might have left town to escape financial problems. Alternately, they had suggested that she might have killed herself with an overdose of drugs; she had overdosed two months before her disappearance, it was said.

Prosecutors were convinced that Karen Jo disappeared because Halcomb killed her. One convict, Troy Heath, supposedly wrote a letter in which he detailed what Halcomb had told him about Karen Jo's death. Halcomb, Heath wrote, had chopped up Karen Jo's body in a meat grinder in Missouri and fed the pieces to hogs. Later, Heath disavowed the letter.

Maybe that is what happened to Karen Jo. Halcomb, it was known, dodged his parole officer for two days while driving to California and back to Indianapolis. That would have made a trip through Missouri possible.

At any rate, Halcomb, who had hoped to commit the perfect murder, instead ended up being sentenced to ninety-five years in prison to ponder how it had all happened without the discovery of his ex-wife's corpse. To this day, nobody knows for sure what happened to Karen Jo's body.

# The Case of the Missing Clerk

Had Indianapolis police ever discovered the mystery man with the mustache, considered one of the last persons seen with Lydia Edna Fowler, they might have learned what happened to her. But they didn't. So, the killing of the seventeen-year-old bank clerk from New Whiteland was never solved.

Lydia's partly decomposed body was found near a culvert in southwestern Marion County on November 10, 1959, by two hunters taking advantage of the first day of the season. She had been dead about a month, last seen the night of October 8.

The body was without shoes and was clad in torn nylon hose, a gray skirt and a blue sweater. The sweater had been pulled up to her shoulders, and one bra strap was broken. Her skirt and underclothing were intact. Her shoes, purse, bowling shirt, locket, watch and coat were missing and never found; it was too cool at the time of the year for her to have been coatless. She wore a diamond engagement ring and a 1959 Center Grove High School ring. Bloodstains on the railing of the concrete culvert above her suggested that the body had been dropped some twelve feet.

The autopsy showed that Lydia had suffered a crushed head, five broken ribs and a broken right hip and had scratches and road burns on her arms, legs and knees. She had not been sexually assaulted. Police first theorized that she might have been struck by a car, whose driver panicked and threw her over the bridge. But the coroner said that she had been killed by a vicious beating before her body was dumped. It was unlikely that all the injuries she had suffered occurred when her body plummeted to its resting place.

Investigators eliminated her boyfriend as a suspect; he passed a lie detector test. He said he had not seen her since October 3 and that they had broken up because Lydia thought they were getting too serious. He said that Lydia had called him on October 8 and reported that she was being followed by a tall man with a mustache.

The site was near the Circle Theater in downtown Indianapolis. Lydia, who had been a clerk-typist at Indiana National Bank for about five months, had bowled with the bank team earlier in the evening. Her bowling companions said that she had made several telephone calls. About 8:30 p.m. she went to a movie. She planned to be picked up on Monument Circle shortly after midnight by her brother-in-law, to be taken home to New Whiteland, where she stayed with him and her sister. She never showed up, he told police. He had asked a policeman to search Circle Theater for her but got the brush-off; he was told that he could search it himself.

An usher told police that he had seen a man follow Fowler into the theatre and take a seat near her. Later, she was seen sipping a soft drink in the lobby with a man, described as about thirty years old, medium height, with dark hair and a bushy mustache. He wore tan slacks and shirt.

Police believed that Lydia left the theatre with a man, perhaps reluctantly. Once at the deserted location where she was found, police believe that she might have been subjected to unwelcome sexual advances. Because most of her injuries were on her left side, police came to believe she was attacked in a vehicle and hit on the head with a blunt object. She probably died quickly, it was thought. Her assaulter may have thrown the body over the culvert bridge and fled. Police did not rule out the possibility that she had been killed elsewhere and then driven to the remote spot. It was so near the home of her erstwhile boyfriend that investigators mused about whether the location had been chosen to throw suspicion on him.

At one point, a mystery man named "Allen" had been sought as a strong suspect. Fowler's fellow workers said that an "Allen" had called her several times at work, until she said that she didn't wish to talk to him again. The Allen who soon came to police was a thirty-three-year-old adding machine repairman, who admitted that he had met Fowler on a downtown street when she had dropped her purse. They had seen each other only twice, he said, and had gone on one date. He was cleared through a lie detector test.

More than thirty-five people were interrogated. One was an electrician who had tried unsuccessfully to date Fowler. Two suspects were "booked," but evidence was not found to connect them with the crime. Police began to suspect that Fowler had secret romantic liaisons unknown to her friends and relatives.

In bizarre developments, police grew hopeful when a man told them that she had been killed by a group of boys; he gave names and places. Then it was learned that this man was being committed to a mental institution. Authorities even consulted Peter Hurkos, a Dutch psychic living in Wisconsin. Given Lydia Fowler's picture in the high school annual, Hurkos said that she had met a violent death (no news there) but could provide no additional information.

By 1962, police had checked out 117 tips in the death of Lydia Fowler. They made little headway. And they still haven't.

# About the Author

Fred D. Cavinder has written seven books on Indiana topics since 1985. He is retired after thirty-seven years as a reporter, editor and feature writer for the *Indianapolis Star* newspaper, including sixteen years as editor of the paper's Sunday magazine supplement. A 1953 graduate of Indiana University, he has since that time written and taken photographs for numerous regional, state and international publications.

Visit us at
www.historypress.net